Detailed Minutiae of
Soldier Life
in the Army of Northern Virginia
1861–1865

See page 106.

DETAILED MINUTIÆ

OF

SOLDIER LIFE

IN THE

ARMY OF NORTHERN VIRGINIA

1861-1865

BY

CARLTON McCARTHY

PRIVATE SECOND COMPANY RICHMOND HOWITZERS, CUTSHAW'S
BATTALION ARTILLERY, SECOND CORPS, A. N. V.

WITH ILLUSTRATIONS

BY

WM. L. SHEPPARD, Esq.

LIEUTENANT SECOND COMPANY RICHMOND HOWITZERS, A. N V.

Introduction to the Bison Book Edition
by Brian S. Wills

University of Nebraska Press
Lincoln and London

CONTENTS.

INTRODUCTION

By Brian S. Wills

For weeks the army remained in camp. The routine of drill, sentry duty, and other activities droned on tediously. The hours passed so slowly that even the usual diversions such as letter writing and card playing took on an almost oppressive monotony. Finally word filtered through the chain of command to prepare three days' rations and a sense of excitement shuddered through the ranks.

Early the next morning came the marching orders, and although few knew where they were going, virtually all welcomed the break in routine. But the contentment subsided as the column stretched across miles of alternately dusty or muddy roads, through the humidity of sweltering summer days or into the chill of autumn nights. Then, when the plodding foot soldiers thought they might go on forever, came the faint rumbling of distant thunder, over the clank of accoutrements and the thump of marching feet. Word again filtered through the ranks to close up and the pace quickened.

As the men moved farther, the unmistakable sights and sounds of battle increased. The column passed the wounded and dead from earlier fighting, the smell of black powder filling the air. Shifting into line of battle, the men prepared themselves to meet the enemy. For much of the day they did little but wait. Suddenly a line of blue emerged from the woods across the field and started across. Officers shouted orders and the men steeled themselves for combat. As the blue line approached within range, the combatants traded volleys and the lines became obscured in a pall of smoke. When the two forces collided, the fighting devolved into hundreds of individual combats with men choking, stabbing, shooting or clubbing each other. For each the battle was won or lost in this close-hand fighting. As the combat subsided—almost as quickly as it had begun—the blood-streaked, sweat-drenched survivors could collapse in exhaustion knowing that they had won because they had survived. And so, counting the costs by the names that would not answer the next roll call, the unit moved on to other camps, marches, and battles.

This composite sketch typifies the experience of thousands of Americans as their country split asunder and went to war in 1861–65. Families, friends, and whole communities divided as young men marched off to fight a war few thought would last for very long. Yet the fighting dragged on, producing enormous casualties and costing millions of dollars, straining the economic structure and tearing at the social fabric of North and South.

The South, as Confederate States of America, suffered most severely. By the very nature of the conflict much of the fighting occurred on its soil. Southern cities suffered a disproportionate share of destruction. Southern agriculture bore the brunt of sustaining soldiers from both sides as well as the civilians of the region. Yet the experiences of those who fought in the war were universal. Soldiers, North and South, endured disease, hunger, boredom, and countless other hardships and dangers. Much of what can be found in *Detailed Minutiae of Soldier Life in the Army of Northern Virginia* could be applied to men in either uniform. In any event, no one who participated in the crucible of war emerged unscathed or unchanged.

One of these participants was fourteen-year-old Carlton McCarthy. Born in Richmond, Virginia, on August 18, 1847, McCarthy attended school in the city. Still a student when the South seceded, he was too young to join the Confederate Army at the beginning of the war. He had to content himself with watching as his older brother, Edward, went to war, a member of the First Company, Richmond Howitzers. Carlton dedicated this later study of soldier life to the memory of his brother, who fell victim to a sharpshooter's bullet in the bitter fighting at Cold Harbor, Virginia, on June 4, 1864.[1]

Although still too young for the service, Carlton McCarthy joined the Richmond "Home Guard." Finally, in 1864, he became a member of the Second Company of the Richmond Howitzers and remained with that unit until surrendering with Robert E. Lee's Army of Northern Virginia at Appomattox in April 1865.

At the close of the war, McCarthy worked in a variety of professions before establishing himself as a bookseller and publisher. He wrote several books, involved himself in Confederate veterans' activities and became active in local politics. Following an unsuccessful bid for mayor of Richmond in 1902, he won election to that office two years later, unseating long-time incumbent Richard M. Taylor. McCarthy remained in office until 1908 and continued to serve in a variety of public positions before retiring in 1920. He died in Richmond on April 16, 1936.[2]

As an adherent of the South's "Lost Cause" celebrations, McCarthy spent much of his postwar life crusading for the memory of those who fought for the Confederacy. He became involved in preserving the deeds of these soldiers through such memorials as statues and published reminiscences. Much of what would be contained in *Detailed Minutiae* first appeared as a series of "sketches of soldier life" in the *Southern Historical Society Papers* from 1876 to 1879.[3] In 1882, McCarthy published his "sketches" in book form, adding the considerable talents of William L. Sheppard as illustrator.

McCarthy's chief aim was to perpetuate the deeds of the ordinary men who fought for the South. He believed that historians and students of the war had failed to separate the "individual soldier" from the "huge masses of men composing the armies" (p. 1). For McCarthy, this Confederate private was "a perfect, all-enduring, never-tiring and invincible soldier" (p. 16). He was the patriot personified, battling heroically and unfledgingly against insurmountable odds. The struggles and the hardships endured deserved cherished memory.

Such a focus led McCarthy into numerous instances of hyperbole. Even so, much of what he so enthusiastically overstated stemmed from genuine affection for his fellow comrades in arms. Thus, McCarthy proudly asserted that in passing through Southern towns the soldiers "all conducted themselves properly" and that there was "a wonderful absence of stealing or plundering" (p. 62). Yet, civilians frequently complained of being victimized as fully by their own soldiers as by the enemy.

Occasionally these attempts to explain away less flattering aspects of the common soldier's behavior led McCarthy to employ tortured logic. For instance, he observed that "when armed guards were placed over the smokehouses and barns, it was not so much because the commanding general doubted the honesty as that he knew the necessities of his troops" (p. 62). McCarthy also had to admit that when the presence of corn proved too much for the hungry Confederate "his honesty gave way under the pressure. How could he resist? He didn't— he took some roasting ears!" (p. 69).

The highly figurative language of the late nineteenth century marked his choice of words and images. Of the obligation the survivors had to preserve the memory of the fallen, McCarthy explained floridly, "Dying, his head pillowed on the bosom of his mother, Virginia, he heard that his name would be honored" (p. 9). Unquestionably, the author was a product of his times.

In regard to race, McCarthy also belonged to the times. He saw black Southerners through the eyes of one who benefited from a social structure based upon paternalism and white supremacy. His few references to African-Americans reflect attitudes and language common to the period. He maintained that "quite a large number" of men brought a servant with them into the service and concluded, "Never was there fonder admiration than these darkies displayed for their masters" (p. 19).

However, if occasionally yielding to contemporary attitudes, and to the urge to amplify the heroics and minimize the shortcomings of the common soldier, McCarthy also provided much of the rich detail of ordinary experiences "familiar to all soldiers, and by them not thought worthy of mention to others, because of their familiarity" (p. 16). His observations concerning soldier life and human nature offered insights into the personalities and mentalities of men under the peculiar conditions of camp and battle. These observations covered a wide range of topics from the effects of dust, heat, and sand on marching men to the innovative ways in which hungry men satiated their appetites. Nothing of a Civil War soldier's life and experiences was the way in which later generations would conceive them. The battlefield was certainly not the chess board over which men moved with ease. Rather, it was a chaotic mass of humanity, choked by smoke and plagued by poor communications. These conditions severely limited every participant's sense of the ebb and flow of battle; but the private's limitations were particularly acute. He saw only the action that occupied his immediate space and scope of vision. The "fog of war" had real meaning to him.

From these pages emerges a portrait of men being tested, developing their skills of adaptation and endurance. The civilian who evolved into a soldier and survived, came away with a greater sense of himself and others and a greater appreciation for the simple pleasures of life.

Yet, this evolutionary process was hardly a

simple one. The young man who went to war for the first time held an amazing conglomeration of misconceptions. His notions of war bore little similarity to war's reality. He had no practical sense of what it meant to be a soldier and this ignorance made the transition from civilian to soldier difficult. McCarthy noted a number of common "romantic ideas dissipated" by "wisdom, born of experience" (pp. 29, 33).

Indeed, the common soldier had little choice but to educate himself rapidly to the requirements of military service. He required few marches before learning the wisdom of discarding useless or weighty items that he would otherwise have to carry. In camp the early desire to volunteer for even the most grudging or dangerous assignments simply because he was a "soldier" faded as he increasingly offered to do little more than duty demanded. In battle he evolved from recklessly risking himself and from regarding a wound as a "practical benefit" bringing honor, a furlough, or a discharge, to seeking protection and thereby to "guard[ing] his life" (p. 33). Pleasure became relative as the soldier learned to relish the rare moments of plenty in the midst of privation, camaraderie in the face of loneliness, and contentment in the face of hardship.

Although he followed the common soldier into all facets of life in camp, on the march and in battle, McCarthy devoted much of the final portion of his book to his own experiences at the end of and immediately following the war. He detailed the events of the final days of his service with the Second Company, Richmond Howitzers, in the entrenchments at Petersburg, and the retreat to Appomattox. Forced to abandon the artillery pieces they had served, the cannoneers became "improvised infantry" and participated in the fighting at Sailor's Creek before finally surrendering with the remainder of the Army of Northern Virginia.

McCarthy then described his return to Richmond with another comrade. Hungry and penniless, the "survivors" took meals where they could. They were surprised to see that another veteran, General Robert E. Lee, chose the same route from the surrender site. During the march from Appomattox, McCarthy noticed one other recent development. At one of their stops, while they worked for their meals, they were watched by a number of former slaves "now in the full enjoyment of newly conferred liberty, and consequently having no thought of doing any work" (p. 178). The scene reflected the changing conditions wrought by the war and foreshadowed the antagonisms of Reconstruction as black and white Southerners sought to establish new positions in the evolving social structure.

Despite this relatively brief autobiographical section of the book, *Detailed Minutiae* clearly was not designed to memorialize the author's role in the war. McCarthy desired most to make the reader aware of the reality of soldier life in the Civil War. He was determined to "preserve" the "little details" of the soldier's typical experiences (p. 16). Therein lies the great contribution of the book. For his own and subsequent generations, McCarthy portrayed the soldier as a practical-minded human being making the best of often horrendous circumstances. He stripped the artificial glamour attached to war and its participants by those who never experienced its reality.

McCarthy's work was obviously a tribute to the Confederate common soldier, but its insights can be more widely applied. The book deserves its place among the memoirs and reminiscences of the participants on both sides of the conflict. Civil War scholar Bell I. Wiley considered *Detailed Minutiae* "the most interesting and the most informative of all memoirs written by privates," although he cautioned that the author took "a somewhat roseate view of the Confederate Army."[4] Certainly, when coupled with Wiley's classic historical studies of soldier life, *The Life of Johnny Reb* and *The Life of Billy Yank,* and the more recent examinations by Reid Mitchell, Earl Hess, James I. Robertson, Jr., and others, McCarthy's study adds to our understanding of what military service in the Civil War meant to the average private soldier.

NOTES

1. Carlton McCarthy, *Detailed Minutiae of Soldier Life in the Army of Northern Virginia, 1861–1865* (Richmond: Carlton McCarthy and Company, 1882), p. iii. All subsequent page numbers in the text are from the 1882 edition. On the death of Edward McCarthy, see William Meade Dame, *From the Rapidan to Richmond and the Spottsylvania Campaign* (Baltimore: Green-Lucas Company, 1920), pp. 209–10.

2. "McCarthy, 89, Once Mayor, Dies at Home," *Richmond Times Dispatch,* April 17, 1936, pp. 1, 3; "McCarthy Rites Set for 3 P.M.," *Richmond News Leader,* April 17, 1936, p. 2; Christopher Silver, *Twentieth-Century Richmond: Planning, Politics and Race* (Knoxville: University of Tennessee Press, 1984), pp. 44–78 passim; W. Asbury Christian, *Richmond: Her Past and Present* (Richmond: L. H. Jenkins, 1912), pp. 438, 483, 495–513 passim.

3. *Southern Historical Society Papers* 1 (Feb. 1876), pp. 76–89; 2 (Sept. 1876), pp. 129–35; 2 (Nov. 1876), pp. 226–32; 3 (Jan. 1877), pp. 13–19; 6 (July 1878), pp. 1–9; 6 (Nov. 1878), pp. 193–214; 7 (Apr. 1879), pp. 176–85.

4. Bell I. Wiley, *The Life of Johnny Reb: The Common Soldier of the Confederacy* (Baton Rouge: Louisiana State University Press, 1978), p. 424.

5. See Wiley, *Life of Johnny Reb;* Bell I. Wiley, *The Life of Billy Yank: The Common Soldier of the Union* (Baton Rouge: Louisiana State University Press, 1978); James I. Robertson, Jr., *Soldiers: Blue and Gray* (Columbia: University of South Carolina Press, 1988); Reid Mitchell, *Civil War Soldiers* (New York: Viking Penguin, 1988).

SOLDIER LIFE

IN THE

ARMY OF NORTHERN VIRGINIA.

———◆———

CHAPTER I.

A VOICE FROM THE RANKS. — INTRODUCTORY.

WE are familiar with the names and deeds of the "generals," from the commander-in-chief down to the almost innumerable brigadiers, and we are all more or less ignorant of the habits and characteristics of the individuals who composed the rank and file of the "grand armies" of 1861–65.

As time rolls on, the historian, condensing matters, mentions "the men" by brigades, divisions, and corps. But here let us look at the individual soldier separated from the huge masses of men composing the armies, and doing his own work and duty.

The fame of Lee and Jackson, world-wide, and as the years increase ever brighter, is but condensed and personified admiration of the

Confederate soldier, wrung from an unwilling world by his matchless courage, endurance, and devotion. Their fame is an everlasting monument to the mighty deeds of the nameless host who followed them through so much toil and blood to glorious victories.

The weak, as a rule, are borne down by the strong; but that does not prove that the strong are also the right. The weak suffer wrong, learn the bitterness of it, and finally, by resisting it, become the defenders of right and justice. When the mighty nations of the earth oppress the feeble, they nerve the arms and fire the hearts of God's instruments for the restoration of justice; and when one section of a country oppresses and insults another, the result is the pervasive malady, — war! which will work out the health of the nation, or leave it a bloody corpse.

The principles for which the Confederate soldier fought, and in defense of which he died, are to-day the harmony of this country. So long as they were held in abeyance, the country was in turmoil and on the verge of ruin.

It is not fair to demand a reason for actions above reason. The heart is greater than the mind. No man can exactly define the cause for which the Confederate soldier fought. He was above human reason and above human law, secure in his own rectitude of purpose, accountable to God only, having assumed for himself a " nationality," which he was minded to defend with his life and his property, and thereto pledged his sacred honor.

In the honesty and simplicity of his heart, the Confederate soldier had neglected his own interests and rights, until his accumulated wrongs and indignities forced him to one grand, prolonged effort to free himself from the pain of them. He dared not refuse to hear the call to arms, so plain was the duty and so urgent the call. His brethren and friends were answering the bugle-call and the roll of the drum. To stay was dishonor and shame !

He would not obey the dictates of tyranny. To disobey was death. He disobeyed and fought for his life. The romance of war charmed him, and he hurried from the embrace of his mother to the embrace of death. His playmates, his friends, and his associates were gone ; he was lonesome, and he sought a reunion " in camp." He would not receive as gospel the dogmas of fanatics, and so he became a "rebel." Being a rebel, he must be punished. Being punished, he resisted. Resisting, he died.

The Confederate soldier opposed immense odds. In the " seven days battles " around Richmond, 80,000 drove to the James River 115,000 of the enemy. At Fredericksburg, in

1862, 78,000 of them routed 110,000 Federal troops. At Chancellorsville, in 1863, 57,000 under Lee and Jackson whipped, and but for the death of Jackson would have annihilated, an army of 132,000 men, — more than double their own number. At Gettysburg, 62,000 of them assailed the heights manned by 112,000. At the Wilderness, in 1864, 63,000 met and successfully resisted 141,000 of the enemy. At Appomattox, in April, 1865, 8,000 of them surrendered to the host commanded by Grant. The United States government, at the end of the war, mustered out of service 1,000,000 of men, and had in the field, from first to last, 2,600,000. If the Confederate soldier had then had only this disparity of numbers to contend with, he would have driven every invader from the soil of Virginia.

But the Confederate soldier fought, in addition to these odds, the facilities for the transportation and concentration of troops and supplies afforded by the network of railways in the country north of him, all of which were subject to the control of the government, and backed by a treasury which was turning out money by the ton, one dollar of which was equal to sixty Confederate dollars.

It should be remembered also that, while the South was restricted to its own territory for supplies, and its own people for men, the North drew on the world for material, and on every nation of the earth for men.

The arms and ammunition of the Federal soldiers were abundant and good, — so abundant and so good that they supplied *both* armies, and were greatly preferred by Confederate officers. The equipment of the Federal armies was well-nigh perfect. The facilities for manufacture were simply unlimited, and the nation thought no expenditure of treasure too great, if only the country, the *Union!* could be saved. The factory and the foundry chimneys made a pillar of smoke by day and of fire by night. The latest improvements were hurried to the front, and adopted by both armies almost simultaneously; for hardly had the Federal bought, when the Confederate captured, and used, the *very latest*.

Commissary stores were piled up all over Virginia, for the use of the invading armies. They had more than they could protect, and their loss was gain to the hungry defenders of the soil.

The Confederate soldier fought a host of ills occasioned by the deprivation of chloroform and morphia, which were excluded from the Confederacy, by the blockade, as contraband of war. The man who has submitted to amputation without chloroform, or tossed on a couch of

agony for a night and a day without sleep for
the want of a dose of morphia, may possibly be
able to estimate the advantages which resulted
from the possession by the Federal surgeons of
an unlimited supply of these.

The Confederate soldier fought bounties and
regular monthly pay ; the " Stars and Stripes,"
the " Star Spangled Banner," " Hail Columbia," " Tramp, Tramp, Tramp," " John Brown's
Body," " Rally round the Flag," and all the
fury and fanaticism which skilled minds could
create, — opposing this grand array with the
modest and homely refrain of " Dixie," sup-
ported by a mild solution of " Maryland, My
Maryland." He fought good wagons, fat horses,
and tons of quartermaster's stores ; pontoon
trains, of splendid material and construction, by
the mile ; gunboats, wooden and iron, and men-
of-war ; illustrated papers, to cheer the " Boys
in Blue " with sketches of the glorious deeds
they did not do ; Bibles by the car load, and
tracts by the million, — the first to prepare
them for death, and the second to urge upon
them the duty of dying.

The Confederate soldier fought the " Sani-
tary Commission," whose members, armed with
every facility and convenience, quickly carried
the sick and wounded of the Federal army to
comfortable quarters, removed the bloody gar-

ments, laid the sufferer on a clean and dry couch, clothed him in clean things, and fed him on the best the world could afford and money buy.

He fought the well-built, thoroughly equipped ambulances, the countless surgeons, nurses, and hospital stewards, and the best surgical appliances known to the medical world. He fought the commerce of the United States and all the facilities for war which Europe could supply, while his own ports were closed to all the world. He fought the trained army officers and the regular troops of the United States Army, assisted by splendid native volunteer soldiers, besides swarms of men, the refuse of the earth, — Portuguese, Spanish, Italian, German, Irish, Scotch, English, French, Chinese, Japanese, — white, black, olive, and brown. He laid down life for life with this hireling host, who died for pay, mourned by no one, missed by no one, loved by no one; who were better fed and clothed, fatter, happier, and more contented in the army than ever they were at home, and whose graves strew the earth in lonesome places, where none go to weep. When one of these fell, two could be bought to fill the gap. The Confederate soldier killed these without compunction, and their comrades buried them without a tear.

The Confederate soldier fought the cries of

distress which came from his home, — tales of
woe, want, insult, and robbery. He fought men
who knew that *their* homes (when they had
any) were safe, their wives and children, their
parents and sisters, sheltered, and their business
affairs more than usually prosperous ; who could
draw sight drafts, have them honored, and make
the camp table as bountiful and luxurious as
that of a New York hotel. He fought a government founded by the genius of his fathers,
which derived its strength from principles they
formulated, and which persuaded its soldiers
that they were the champions of the constitu-
tional liberty which they were marching to in-
vade, and eventually to destroy.

The relative strength of armies becomes a
matter of secondary importance when these
facts are considered. The disparity of numbers
only, would never have produced the result
which the combination of these various forces
did, — the surrender of the Army of Northern
Virginia.

The Confederate soldier was purely patriotic.
He foresaw clearly, and deliberately chose, the
trials which he endured. He was an individual
who could not become the indefinite portion of
a mass, but fought for himself, on his own account. He was a self-sacrificing hero, but did
not claim that distinction or any merit, feeling

only that he was in the line of duty to self, country, and God. He fought for a principle, and needed neither driving nor urging, but was eager and determined to fight. He was not a politic man, but a man under fervent feeling, forgetful of the possibilities and calamities of war, pressing his claims to the rights of humanity.

The Confederate soldier was a monomaniac for four years. His mania was, the independence of the Confederates States of America, secured by force of arms.

The Confederate soldier was a venerable old man, a youth, a child, a preacher, a farmer, merchant, student, statesman, orator, father, brother, husband, son, — the wonder of the world, the terror of his foes!

If the peace of this country can only be preserved by forgetting the Confederate soldier's deeds and his claims upon the South, the blessing is too dearly bought. We have sworn to be grateful to him. Dying, his head pillowed on the bosom of his mother, Virginia, he heard that his name would be honored.

When we fill up, hurriedly, the bloody chasm opened by war, we should be careful that we do not bury therein many noble deeds, some tender memories, some grand examples, and some hearty promises washed with tears.

The following letter, written by an aged father to his only son, then a mere boy, who had
volunteered as an infantry soldier and was already in the field, is an appropriate conclusion
to this chapter; showing admirably well the
kind of inspiration which went from Southern
homes to Southern soldiers: —

AT HOME, *July* 17, 1861.

MY DEAR SON, — It may have seemed strange to
you that a professing Christian father so freely gave
you, a Christian son, to enlist in the volunteer service. My reason was that I regarded this as a *purely
defensive war.* Not only did the Southern Confederacy propose to adjust the pending difficulties by
peaceful and equitable negotiations, but Virginia used
again and again the most earnest and noble efforts to
prevent a resort to the sword. These overtures having been proudly spurned, and our beloved South
having been threatened with invasion and subjugation,
it seemed to me that nothing was left us but stern
resistance, or abject submission, to unconstitutional
power. A brave and generous people could not for
a moment hesitate between such alternatives. A war
in defense of our homes and firesides, of our wives
and children, of all that makes life worth possess-
ing, is the result. While I most deeply deplored the
necessity for the sacrifice, I could not but rejoice that
I had a son to offer to the service of the country, and
if I had a dozen, *I would most freely give them all.*
As you are now cheerfully enduring the hardships of

the camp, I know you will listen to a father's suggestions touching the duties of your new mode of life.

1. Take special care of your health. More soldiers die of disease than in battle. A thin piece of damp sponge in the crown of your hat during exposure to the hot sun, the use of thick shoes and a water-proof coat in rainy weather, the practice of drinking cold water when you are very warm as slowly as you sip hot tea, the thorough mastication of your food, the avoiding of damp tents and damp grounds during sleep, and frequent ablutions of your person are all the hints I can give you on this point. Should you need anything that I can supply, let me hear from you. I will do what I can to make you comfortable. After all, you must learn to endure hardness as a good soldier. Having never slept a single night in your whole life except in a pleasant bed, and never known a scarcity of good food, you doubtless find the ways of the camp rough ; but never mind. The war, I trust, will soon be over, and then the remembrance of your hardships will sweeten the joy of peace.

2. The rules of war require prompt and unquestioning obedience. You may sometimes think the command arbitrary and the officer supercilious, but *it is yours to obey*. An undisciplined army is a curse to its friends and a derision to its foes. Give your whole influence, therefore, to the maintenance of lawful authority and of strict order. Let your superiors feel assured that whatever they entrust to *you* will be faithfully done. Composed of such soldiers, and led

by skillful and brave commanders, our army, by the blessing of God, will never be defeated. It is, moreover, engaged in a holy cause, and must triumph.

3. Try to maintain your Christian profession among your comrades. I need not caution you against strong drink as useless and hurtful, nor against profanity, so common among soldiers. Both these practices you abhor. Aim to take at once a decided stand for God. If practicable have prayers regularly in your tent, or unite with your fellow-disciples in prayer-meetings in the camp. Should preaching be accessible, always be a hearer. Let the world know that you are a Christian. Read a chapter in the New Testament, which your mother gave you, every morning and evening, when you can, and engage in secret prayer to God for his holy Spirit to guide and sustain you. I would rather hear of your death than of the shipwreck of your faith and good conscience.

4. As you will come into habitual contact with men of every grade, make special associates only of those whose influence on your character is felt to be good. Some men love to tell extravagant stories, to indulge in vulgar wit, to exult in a swaggering carriage, to pride themselves on their coarse manners, to boast of their heroism, and to give utterance to feelings of revenge against the enemy. All this is injurious to young and impressible minds. If you admire such things, you will insensibly imitate them, and imitation will work gradual but certain detriment to your character. Other men are refined without being affected.

They can relax into occasional pleasantries without violating modesty. They can be loyal to their government without indulging private hatred against her foes. They can be cool and brave in battle, and not be braggarts in the absence of danger. Above all, they can be humble, spiritual, and active Christians, and yet mingle in the stirring and perilous duties of soldier-life. Let these be your companions and models. You will thus return from the dangers of camp without a blemish on your name.

5. Should it be your lot to enter into an engagement with the enemy, lift up your heart in secret ejaculations to the ever-present and good Being, that He will protect you from sudden death, or if you fall, that He will receive your departing spirit, cleansed in the blood of Jesus, into His kingdom. It is better to trust in the Lord than to put confidence in princes. Commit your eternal interests, therefore, to the keeping of the Almighty Saviour. You should not, even in the hour of deadly conflict, cherish personal rage against the enemy, any more than an officer of the law hates the victim of the law. How often does a victorious army tenderly care for the dead and wounded of the vanquished. War is a tremendous scourge which Providence sometimes uses to chastise proud and wicked nations. Both parties must suffer, even though one may get the advantage. There is no occasion then for adding to the intrinsic evils of the system the odious feature of animosity to individuals. In the ranks of the foe are thousands of plain men who do not understand the principles for

which we are struggling. They are deceived by artful demagogues into a posture of hostility to those whom, knowing, they would love. It is against such men that you may perhaps be arrayed, and the laws of war do not forbid you to pity them even in the act of destroying them. It is the more important that *we* should exhibit a proper temper in this unfortunate contest, because many professed Christians and ministers of the gospel at the North are breathing out, in their very prayers and sermons, threatenings and slaughter against us. Oh! how painful that a gray-headed pastor should publicly exclaim, " *I would hang them as quick as I would shoot a mad dog !* "

6. Providence has placed you in the midst of thoughtless and unpardoned men. What a beautiful thing it would be if you could win some of them to the Saviour. Will you not try? You will have many opportunities of saying a word in season. The sick you may comfort, the wavering you may confirm, the backslidden you may reclaim, the weary and heavy laden you may point to Jesus for rest to the soul. It is not presumptuous for a young man kindly and meekly to commend the gospel to his brother soldiers. The hardest of them will not repel a gentle approach, made in private. And many of them would doubtless be glad to have the subject introduced to them. They desire to hear of Jesus, but they lack courage to inquire of his people. An unusually large proportion of pious men have entered the army, and I trust they will give a new complexion to military life. Let them search out each other, and establish a fraternity

among all the worshipers of God. To interchange religious views and administer brotherly counsel will be mutually edifying. "He that watereth shall be watered also himself."

And now, as a soldier has but little leisure, I will not occupy you longer. Be assured that every morning and evening we remember you, at the family altar, to our Father in Heaven. We pray for "a speedy, just, and honorable peace," and for the safe return of all the volunteers to their loved homes. All the children speak often of "brother," and hear your letters read with intense interest. That God Almighty may be your shield and your exceeding great reward, is the constant prayer of your loving father.

CHAPTER II.

THE OUTFIT MODIFIED.

WITH the men who composed the Army of Northern Virginia will die the memory of those little things which made the Confederate soldier peculiarly what he was.

The historian who essays to write the " grand movements " will hardly stop to tell how the hungry private fried his bacon, baked his biscuit, and smoked his pipe ; how he was changed from time to time by the necessities of the service, until the gentleman, the student, the merchant, the mechanic, and the farmer were merged into a perfect, all-enduring, never-tiring and invincible soldier. To preserve these little details, familiar to all soldiers, and by them not thought worthy of mention to others, because of their familiarity, but still dear to them and always the substance of their " war talks," is the object of this book.

The volunteer of 1861 made extensive preparations for the field. Boots, he thought, were an absolute necessity, and the heavier the soles and longer the tops the better. His pants were

THE OUTFIT OF 1861.

stuffed inside the tops of his boots, of course. A double-breasted coat, heavily wadded, with two rows of big brass buttons and a long skirt, was considered comfortable. A small stiff cap, with a narrow brim, took the place of the comfortable "felt," or the shining and towering tile worn in civil life.

Then over all was a huge overcoat, long and heavy, with a cape reaching nearly to the waist. On his back he strapped a knapsack containing a full stock of underwear, soap, towels, comb, brush, looking-glass, tooth-brush, paper and envelopes, pens, ink, pencils, blacking, photographs, smoking and chewing tobacco, pipes, twine string, and cotton strips for wounds and other emergencies, needles and thread, buttons, knife, fork, and spoon, and many other things as each man's idea of what he was to encounter varied. On the outside of the knapsack, solidly folded, were two great blankets and a rubber or oil-cloth. This knapsack, etc., weighed from fifteen to twenty-five pounds, sometimes even more. All seemed to think it was impossible to have on too many or too heavy clothes, or to have too many conveniences, and each had an idea that to be a good soldier he must be provided against every possible emergency.

In addition to the knapsack, each man had a haversack, more or less costly, some of cloth

2

and some of fine morocco, and stored with provisions always, as though he expected any moment to receive orders to march across the Great Desert, and supply his own wants on the way. A canteen was considered indispensable, and at the outset it was thought prudent to keep it full of water. Many, expecting terrific hand-to-hand encounters, carried revolvers, and even bowie-knives. Merino shirts (and flannel) were thought to be the right thing, but experience demonstrated the contrary. Gloves were also thought to be very necessary and good things to have in winter time, the favorite style being buck gauntlets with long cuffs.

In addition to each man's private luggage, each mess, generally composed of from five to ten men, drawn together by similar tastes and associations, had *its* outfit, consisting of a large camp chest containing skillet, frying pan, coffee boiler, bucket for lard, coffee box, salt box, sugar box, meal box, flour box, knives, forks, spoons, plates, cups, etc., etc. These chests were so large that eight or ten of them filled up an army wagon, and were so heavy that two strong men had all they could do to get one of them into the wagon. In addition to the chest each mess owned an axe, water bucket, and bread tray. Then the tents of each company, and little sheet-iron stoves, and stove pipe, and the trunks and valises of the company officers, made an immense pile of stuff, so that each company had a small wagon train of its own.

All thought money to be absolutely necessary, and for awhile rations were disdained and the mess supplied with the best that could be bought with the mess fund. Quite a large number had a " boy " along to do the cooking and washing. Think of it ! a Confederate soldier with a body servant all his own, to bring him a drink of water, black his boots, dust his clothes, cook his corn bread and bacon, and put wood on his fire. Never was there fonder admiration than these darkies displayed for their masters. Their chief delight and glory was to praise the courage and good looks of " Mahse Tom," and prophesy great things about his future. Many a ringing laugh and shout of fun originated in the queer remarks, shining countenance, and glistening teeth of this now forever departed character.

It is amusing to think of the follies of the early part of the war, as illustrated by the outfits of the volunteers. They were so heavily clad, and so burdened with all manner of things, that a march was torture, and the wagon trains were so immense in proportion to the number of troops, that it would have been impossible to guard them in an enemy's country. Subor-

dinate officers thought themselves entitled to
transportation for trunks, mattresses, and fold-
ing bedsteads, and the privates were as ridiculous in their demands.

Thus much by way of introduction. The
change came rapidly, and stayed not until the
transformation was complete. Nor was this
change attributable alone to the orders of the
general officers. The men soon learned the
inconvenience and danger of so much luggage,
and, as they became more experienced, they vied
with each other in reducing themselves to light-
marching trim.

Experience soon demonstrated that boots
were not agreeable on a long march. They
were heavy and irksome, and when the heels
were worn a little one-sided, the wearer would
find his ankle twisted nearly out of joint by
every unevenness of the road. When thoroughly wet, it was a laborious undertaking to
get them off, and worse to get them on in time
to answer the morning roll-call. And so, good,
strong brogues or brogans, with broad bottoms
and big, flat heels, succeeded the boots, and
were found much more comfortable and agreeable, easier put on and off, and altogether the
more sensible.

A short-waisted and single-breasted jacket
usurped the place of the long-tailed coat, and

became universal. The enemy noticed this peculiarity, and called the Confederates gray jackets, which name was immediately transferred to those lively creatures which were the constant admirers and inseparable companions of the Boys in Gray and in Blue.

Caps were destined to hold out longer than some other uncomfortable things, but they finally yielded to the demands of comfort and common sense, and a good soft felt hat was worn instead. A man who has never been a soldier does not know, nor indeed can know, the amount of comfort there is in a good soft hat in camp, and how utterly useless is a " soldier hat " as they are generally made. Why the Prussians, with all their experience, wear their heavy, unyielding helmets, and the French their little caps, is a mystery to a Confederate who has enjoyed the comfort of an old slouch.

Overcoats an inexperienced man would think an absolute necessity for men exposed to the rigors of a northern Virginia winter, but they grew scarcer and scarcer; they were found to be a great inconvenience. The men came to the conclusion that the trouble of carrying them on hot days outweighed the comfort of having them when the cold day arrived. Besides they found that life in the open air hardened them to such an extent that changes in the temperature were not felt to any degree. Some clung to their overcoats to the last, but the majority got tired lugging them around, and either discarded them altogether, or trusted to capturing one about the time it would be needed. Nearly every overcoat in the army in the latter years was one of Uncle Sam's captured from his boys.

The knapsack vanished early in the struggle. It was inconvenient to " change " the underwear too often, and the disposition not to change grew, as the knapsack was found to gall the back and shoulders, and weary the man before half the march was accomplished. The better way was to dress out and out, and wear that outfit until the enemy's knapsacks, or the folks at home supplied a change. Certainly it did not pay to carry around clean clothes while waiting for the time to use them.

Very little washing was done, as a matter of course. Clothes once given up were parted with forever. There were good reasons for this: cold water would not cleanse them or destroy the vermin, and hot water was not always to be had. One blanket to each man was found to be as much as could be carried, and amply sufficient for the severest weather. This was carried generally by rolling it lengthwise, with the rubber cloth outside, tying the ends of the roll together, and throwing the loop thus made over

the left shoulder with the ends fastened together hanging under the right arm.

The haversack held its own to the last, and
was found practical and useful. It very seldom, however, contained rations, but was used
to carry all the articles generally carried in
the knapsack; of course the stock was small.
Somehow or other, many men managed to do
without the haversack, and carried absolutely
nothing but what they wore and had in their
pockets.

The infantry threw away their heavy cap
boxes and cartridge boxes, and carried their
caps and cartridges in their pockets. Canteens
were very useful at times, but they were as a
general thing discarded. They were not much
used to carry water, but were found useful when
the men were driven to the necessity of foraging, for conveying buttermilk, cider, sorghum,
etc., to camp. A good strong tin cup was found
better than a canteen, as it was easier to fill at a
well or spring, and was serviceable as a boiler
for making coffee when the column halted for
the night.

Revolvers were found to be about as useless
and heavy lumber as a private soldier could
carry, and early in the war were sent home to
be used by the women and children in protecting themselves from insult and violence at the

hands of the ruffians who prowled about the country shirking duty.

Strong cotton was adopted in place of flannel and merino, for two reasons: first, because easier to wash; and second, because the vermin did not propagate so rapidly in cotton as in wool. Common white cotton shirts and drawers proved the best that could be used by the private soldier.

Gloves to any but a mounted man were found useless, worse than useless. With the gloves on, it was impossible to handle an axe, buckle harness, load a musket, or handle a rammer at the piece. Wearing them was found to be simply a habit, and so, on the principle that the less luggage the less labor, *they* were discarded.

The camp-chest soon vanished. The brigadiers and major-generals, even, found them too troublesome, and soon they were left entirely to the quartermasters and commissaries. One skillet and a couple of frying pans, a bag for flour or meal, another bag for salt, sugar, and coffee, divided by a knot tied between, served the purpose as well. The skillet passed from mess to mess. Each mess generally owned a frying pan, but often one served a company. The oil-cloth was found to be as good as the wooden tray for making up the dough. The water bucket held its own to the last!

Tents were *rarely seen*. All the poetry about the "*tented field*" died. Two men slept together, each having a blanket and an oil-cloth; one oil-cloth went next to the ground. The two

laid on this, covered themselves with two blankets, protected from the rain with the second oil-cloth on top, and slept very comfortably through rain, snow or hail, as it might be.

Very little money was seen in camp. The men did not expect, did not care for, or often get any pay, and they were not willing to deprive the old folks at home of their little supply, so they learned to do without any money.

When rations got short and were getting shorter, it became necessary to dismiss the darkey servants. Some, however, became company servants, instead of private institutions, and held

out faithfully to the end, cooking the rations
away in the rear, and at the risk of life carrying them to the line of battle to their "young
mahsters."

Reduced to the minimum, the private soldier
consisted of one man, one hat, one jacket, one
shirt, one pair of pants, one pair of drawers, one
pair of shoes, and one pair of socks. His baggage

was one blanket, one rubber blanket, and one
haversack. The haversack generally contained
smoking tobacco and a pipe, and a small piece
of soap, with temporary additions of apples,
persimmons, blackberries, and such other com-
modities as he could pick up on the march.

The company property consisted of two or
three skillets and frying pans, which were sometimes carried in the wagon, but oftener in the
hands of the soldiers. The infantry-men generally preferred to stick the handle of the frying
pan in the barrel of a musket, and so carry it.

The wagon trains were devoted entirely to

the transportation of ammunition and commissary and quartermaster's stores, which had not been issued. Rations which had become company property, and the baggage of the men, when they had any, was carried by the men themselves. If, as was sometimes the case, three days' rations were issued at one time and the troops ordered to cook them, and be prepared to march, they did cook them, *and eat them if possible*, so as to avoid the labor of carrying them. It was not such an undertaking either, to eat three days' rations in one, as frequently none had been issued for more than a day, and when issued were cut down one half.

The infantry found out that bayonets were not of much use, and did not hesitate to throw them, with the scabbard, away.

The artillerymen, who started out with heavy sabres hanging to their belts, stuck them up in the mud as they marched, and left them for the ordnance officers to pick up and turn over to the cavalry.

The cavalrymen found sabres very tiresome when swung to the belt, and adopted the plan of fastening them to the saddle on the left side, with the hilt in front and in reach of the hand. Finally sabres got very scarce even among the cavalrymen, who relied more and more on their short rifles.

No soldiers ever marched with less to encumber them, and none marched faster or held out longer.

The courage and devotion of the men rose equal to every hardship and privation, and the very intensity of their sufferings became a source of merriment. Instead of growling and deserting, they laughed at their own bare feet, ragged clothes and pinched faces; and weak, hungry, cold, wet, worried with vermin and itch, dirty, with no hope of reward or rest, marched cheerfully to meet the well-fed and warmly clad hosts of the enemy.

CHAPTER III.

ROMANTIC IDEAS DISSIPATED.

To offer a man promotion in the early part of the war was equivalent to an insult. The higher the social position, the greater the wealth, the more patriotic it would be to serve in the humble position of a private; and many men of education and ability in the various professions, refusing promotion, served under the command of men greatly their inferiors, mentally, morally, and as soldiers. It soon became apparent that the country wanted knowledge and ability, as well as muscle and endurance, and those who had capacity to serve in higher positions were promoted. Still it remained true that inferior men commanded their superiors in every respect, save one — rank; and leaving out the one difference of rank, the officers and men were about on a par.

It took years to teach the educated privates in the army that it was their duty to give unquestioning obedience to officers because they were such, who were awhile ago their playmates and associates in business. It frequently happened that the private, feeling hurt by the stern authority of the officer, would ask him to one side, challenge him to personal combat, and thrash him well. After awhile these privates learned all about extra duty, half rations, and courts-martial.

It was only to conquer this independent resistance of discipline that punishment or force was necessary. The privates were as willing and anxious to fight and serve as the officers, and needed no pushing up to their duty. It is amusing to recall the disgust with which the men would hear of their assignment to the rear as reserves. They regarded the order as a deliberate insult, planned by some officer who had a grudge against their regiment or battery, who had adopted this plan to prevent their presence in battle, and thus humiliate them. How soon did they learn the sweetness of a day's repose in the rear!

Another romantic notion which for awhile possessed the boys was that soldiers should not try to be comfortable, but glory in getting wet, being cold, hungry, and tired. So they refused shelter in houses or barns, and "like true soldiers" paddled about in the mud and rain, thinking thereby to serve their country better. The real troubles had not come, and they were in a hurry to suffer some. They had not long thus impatiently to wait, nor could they latterly complain of the want of a chance " to do or die." Volunteering for perilous or very onerous duty was popular at the outset, but as duties of this kind thickened it began to be thought time enough when the "orders" were peremptory, or the orderly read the "detail."

Another fancy idea was that the principal occupation of a soldier should be actual conflict with the enemy. They did n't dream of such a thing as camping for six months at a time without firing a gun, or marching and countermarching to mislead the enemy, or driving wagons and ambulances, building bridges, currying horses, and the thousand commonplace duties of the soldier.

On the other hand, great importance was attached to some duties which soon became mere drudgery. Sometimes the whole detail for guard — first, second, and third relief — would make it a point of honor to sit up the entire night, and watch and listen as though the enemy might pounce upon them at any moment, and hurry them off to prison. Of course they soon learned how sweet it was, after two hours' walking of the beat, to turn in for *four hours!* which seemed to the sleepy man an eternity in anticipation, but only a brief time in retrospect, when the corporal gave him a

" chunk," and remarked, " Time to go on guard."

Everybody remembers how we used to talk about " one Confederate whipping a dozen

FALL IN HERE THIRD RELIEF!

Yankees." Literally true sometimes, but, generally speaking, two to one made hard work for the boys. They did n't know at the beginning anything about the advantage the enemy had in being able to present man for man in front and then send as many more to worry the flanks and rear. They learned something about this very soon, and had to contend against it on almost every field they won.

Wounds were in great demand after the first wounded hero made his appearance. His wound was the envy of thousands of unfortunates who had not so much as a scratch to boast, and who felt "small" and of little consequence before the man with a bloody bandage.   Many became despondent and groaned as they thought that perchance after all they were doomed to go home safe and sound, and hear, for all time, the praises of the fellow who had lost his arm by a cannon shot, or had his face ripped by a sabre, or his head smashed with a fragment of shell.   After awhile the wound was regarded as a practical benefit.   It secured a furlough of indefinite length, good eating, the attention and admiration of the fair, and, if permanently disabling, a discharge.   Wisdom, born of experience, soon taught all hands better sense, and the fences and trees and ditches and rocks became valuable, and eagerly sought after when "the music" of "minie" and the roar of the "Napoleon" twelve-pounders was heard.   Death on the field, glorious first and last, was dared for duty's sake, but the good soldier learned to guard his life, and yield it only at the call of duty.

Only the wisest men, those who had seen war before, imagined that the war would last more than a few months.   The young volunteers thought one good battle would settle the whole matter; and, indeed, after "first Manassas"

3

many thought they might as well go home!
The whole North was frightened, and no more
armies would dare assail the soil of Old Virginia.   Colonels and brigadiers, with flesh
wounds not worthy of notice, rushed to Richmond to report the victory and the end of the
war!   They had "seen sights" in the way of
wounded and killed, plunder, etc., and according
to their views, no sane people would try again
to conquer the heroes of that remarkable day.

The newspaper men delighted in telling the
soldiers that the Yankees were a diminutive
race, of feeble constitution, timid as hares, with
no enthusiasm, and that they would perish in
short order under the glow of our southern sun.
Any one who has seen a regiment from Ohio or
Maine knows how true these statements were.
And besides, the newspapers did not mention
the English, Irish, German, French, Italian,
Spanish, Swiss, Portuguese, and negroes, who
were to swell the numbers of the enemy, and as
our army grew less make his larger.   True,
there was not much fight in all this rubbish, but
they answered well enough for drivers of wagons and ambulances, guarding stores and lines
of communication, and doing all sorts of duty,
while the good material was doing the fighting.
Sherman's army, marching through Richmond
after the surrender of Lee and Johnston,

AN EARLY HERO. 1861.

seemed to be composed of a race of giants, well-fed and well-clad.

Many feared the war would end before they would have a fair chance to "make a record," and that when "the cruel war was over" they would have to sit by, dumb, and hear the more fortunate ones, who had "smelt the battle," tell to admiring home circles the story of the bloody field. Most of these "got in" in time to satisfy their longings, and "got out" to learn that the man who did not go, but "kept out," and made money, was more admired and courted than the "poor fellow" with one leg or arm less than is "allowed."

It is fortunate for those who "skulked" that the war ended as it did, for had the South been successful, the soldiers would have been favored with every mark of distinction and honor, and they "despised and rejected," as they deserved to be. While the war lasted it was the delight of some of the stoutly built fellows to go home for a few days, and kick and cuff and tongue-lash the able-bodied bomb-proofs. How coolly and submissively they took it all! How "big" they are now!

The rubbish accumulated by the hope of recognition burdened the soldiers nearly to the end. England was to abolish the blockade and send us immense supplies of fine arms, large and small. France was thinking about landing an imperial force in Mexico, and marching thence to the relief of the South. But the "Confederate yell" never had an echo in the "Marseillaise," or "God save the Queen;" and Old Dixie was destined to sing her own song, without the help even of "Maryland, my Maryland." The "war with England," which was to give Uncle Sam trouble and the South an ally, never came.

Those immense balloons which somebody was always inventing, and which were to sail over the enemy's camps dropping whole cargoes of explosives, never "tugged" at their anchors, or "sailed majestically away."

As discipline improved and the men began to feel that they were no longer simply volunteers, but *enlisted volunteers*, the romantic devotion which they had felt was succeeded by a feeling of constraint and necessity, and while the army was in reality very much improved and strengthened by the change, the soldiers imagined the contrary to be the case. And if discipline had been pushed to too great an extent, the army would have been deprived of the very essence of its life and power.

When the officers began to assert superiority by withdrawing from the messes and organizing "officers' messes," the bond of brotherhood was weakened; and who will say that the dignity which was thus maintained was compensation for the loss of personal devotion as between comrades?

At the outset, the fact that men were in the same company put them somewhat on the same level, and produced an almost perfect bond of sympathy; but as time wore on, the various peculiarities and weaknesses of the men showed themselves, and each company, as a community, separated into distinct circles, as indifferent to each other, save in the common cause, as though they had never met as friends.

The pride of the volunteers was sorely tried by the incoming of conscripts, — the most despised class in the army, — and their devotion to company and regiment was visibly lessened. They could not bear the thought of having these men for comrades, and felt the flag insulted when claimed by one of them as " his flag." It was a great source of annoyance to the true men, but was a necessity. Conscripts crowded together in companies, regiments, and brigades would have been useless, but scattered here and there among the good men, were utilized. And so, gradually, the pleasure that men had in being associated with others whom they respected as equals was taken away, and the social aspect of army life seriously marred.

The next serious blow to romance was the abolishment of elections, and the appointment of officers. Instead of the privilege and pleasure of picking out some good-hearted, brave comrade and making him captain, the lieutenant was promoted without the consent of the men, or, what was harder to bear, some officer hitherto unknown was sent to take command. This was no doubt better for the service, but it had a serious effect on the minds of volunteer patriot soldiers, and looked to them too much like arbitrary power exercised over men who were fighting that very principle. They frequently had to acknowledge, however, that the officers were all they could ask, and in many instances became devotedly attached to them.

As the companies were decimated by disease, wounds, desertions, and death, it became necessary to consolidate them, and the social pleasures received another blow. Men from the same neighborhoods and villages, who had been schoolmates together, were no longer in companies, but mingled indiscriminately with all sorts of men from anywhere and everywhere.

Those who have not served in the army as privates can form no idea of the extent to which such changes as those just mentioned affect the

spirits and general worth of a soldier. Men
who, when surrounded by their old companions,
were brave and daring soldiers, full of spirit
and hope, when thrust among strangers for
whom they cared not, and who cared not for
them, became dull and listless, lost their courage, and were slowly but surely " demoralized."
They did, it is true, in many cases, stand up to
the last, but they did it on dry principle, having
none of that enthusiasm and delight in duty
which once characterized them.

The Confederate soldier was peculiar in that
he was ever ready to fight, but never ready
to submit to the routine duty and discipline
of the camp or the march. The soldiers were
determined to be soldiers after their own notions, and do their duty, for the love of it, as
they thought best. The officers saw the necessity for doing otherwise, and so the conflict
was commenced and maintained to the end.

It is doubtful whether the Southern soldier
would have submitted to any hardships which
were purely the result of discipline, and, on the
other hand, no amount of hardship, clearly of
necessity, could cool his ardor. And in spite of
all this antagonism between the officers and men,
the presence of conscripts, the consolidation of
commands, and many other discouraging facts,
the privates in the ranks so conducted them-

selves that the historians of the North were forced to call them the finest body of infantry ever assembled.

But to know the men, we must see them divested of all their false notions of soldier life, and enduring the incomparable hardships which marked the latter half of the war.

CHAPTER IV.

ON THE MARCH.

IT is a common mistake of those who write on subjects familiar to themselves, to omit the details, which, to one not so conversant with the matters discussed, are necessary to a clear appreciation of the meaning of the writer. This mistake is fatal when the writer lives and writes in one age and his readers live in another. And so a soldier, writing for the information of the citizen, should forget his own familiarity with the every-day scenes of soldier life and strive to record even those things which seem to him too common to mention.

Who does not know all about the marching of soldiers? Those who have never marched with them and some who have. The varied experience of thousands would not tell the whole story of the march. Every man must be heard before the story is told, and even then the part of those who fell by the way is wanting.

Orders to move! Where? when? what for? — are the eager questions of the men as they begin their preparations to march. Generally nobody can answer, and the journey is commenced in utter ignorance of where it is to end. But shrewd guesses are made, and scraps of information will be picked up on the way. The main thought must be to "get ready to move." The orderly sergeant is shouting "Fall in!" and there is no time to lose. The probability is that before you get your blanket rolled up,

find your frying pan, haversack, axe, etc., and "fall in," the roll-call will be over, and some " extra duty" provided.

No wonder there is bustle in the camp. Rapid decisions are to be made between the various conveniences which have accumulated, for some must be left. One fellow picks up the skillet, holds it awhile, mentally determining

how much it weighs, and what will be the
weight of it after carrying it five miles, and reluctantly, with a half-ashamed, sly look, drops
it and takes his place in ranks. Another having added to his store of blankets too freely,
now has to decide which of the two or three he
will leave. The old water-bucket looks large
and heavy, but one stout-hearted, strong-armed
man has taken it affectionately to his care.

This is the time to say farewell to the bread-
tray, farewell to the little piles of clean straw
laid between two logs, where it was so easy to
sleep; farewell to those piles of wood, cut with
so much labor; farewell to the girls in the
neighborhood ; farewell to the spring, farewell
to " our tree " and " our fire," good-by to the
fellows who are not going, and a general good-
by to the very hills and valleys.

Soldiers commonly threw away the most valuable articles they possessed. Blankets, overcoats, shoes, bread and meat, — all gave way
to the necessities of the march; and what one
man threw away would frequently be the very
article that another wanted and would immediately pick up; so there was not much lost
after all.

The first hour or so of the march was generally quite orderly, the men preserving their
places in ranks and marching in solid column ;

but soon some lively fellow whistles an air, somebody else starts a song, the whole column breaks out with roars of laughter; "route step" takes the place of order, and the jolly singing, laughing, talking, and joking that follows no one could describe.

Now let any young officer who sports a new hat, coat, saddle, or anything odd, or fine, dare to pass along, and how nicely he is attended to. The expressions of good-natured fun, or contempt, which one regiment of infantry was capable of uttering in a day for the benefit of such passers-by, would fill a volume. As one thing or another in the dress of the "subject" of their remarks attracted attention, they would shout, "Come out of that hat! — you can't hide in thar!" "Come out of that coat, come out — there's a man in it!" "Come out of them boots!" The infantry seemed to know exactly what to say to torment cavalry and artillery, and generally said it. If any one on the roadside was simple enough to recognize and address by name a man in the ranks, the whole column would kindly respond, and add all sorts of pleasant remarks, such as, "Halloa, John, here's your brother!" "Bill! oh, Bill! here's your ma!" "Glad to see you! How's your grandma?" How d'ye do!" "Come out of that 'biled shirt'!"

Troops on the march were generally so cheerful and gay that an outsider, looking on them as they marched, would hardly imagine how they suffered. In summer time, the dust, combined with the heat, caused great suffering. The nostrils of the men, filled with dust, became dry and feverish, and even the throat did not escape. The "grit" was felt between the teeth, and the eyes were rendered almost useless. There was dust in eyes, mouth, ears, and hair. The shoes were full of sand, and the dust, penetrating the clothes, and getting in at the neck, wrists, and ankles, mixed with perspiration, produced an irritant almost as active as cantharides. The heat was at times terrific, but the men became greatly accustomed to it, and endured it with wonderful ease. Their heavy woolen clothes were a great annoyance; tough linen or cotton clothes would have been a great relief; indeed, there are many objections to woolen clothing for soldiers, even in winter. The sun produced great changes in the appearance of the men: their skins, tanned to a dark brown or red, their hands black almost, and long uncut beard and hair, burned to a strange color, made them barely recognizable to the home folks.

If the dust and the heat were not on hand to annoy, their very able substitutes were: mud, cold, rain, snow, hail and wind took their places. Rain was the greatest discomfort a soldier could have; it was more uncomfortable than the severest cold with clear weather. Wet clothes, shoes, and blankets; wet meat and bread; wet feet and wet ground; wet wood to burn, or rather not to burn; wet arms and ammunition; wet ground to sleep on, mud to wade through, swollen creeks to ford, muddy springs, and a thousand other discomforts attended the rain. There was no comfort on a rainy day or night except in "bed," — that is, under your blanket and oil-cloth. Cold winds, blowing the rain in the faces of the men, increased the discomfort. Mud was often so deep as to submerge the horses and mules, and at times it was necessary for one man or more to extricate another from the mud holes in the road. Night marching was attended with additional discomforts and dangers, such as falling off bridges, stumbling into ditches, tearing the face and injuring the eyes against the bushes and projecting limbs of trees, and getting separated from your own company and hopelessly lost in the multitude. Of course, a man lost had no sympathy. If he dared to ask a question, every man in hearing would answer, each differently, and then the whole multitude would roar with laughter at the lost man, and ask him "if his mother knew he was out?"

Very few men had comfortable or fitting shoes, and fewer had socks, and, as a consequence, the suffering from bruised and inflamed feet was terrible. It was a common practice, on long marches, for the men to take off their shoes and carry them in their hands or swung over the shoulder. Bloody footprints in the snow were not unknown to the soldiers of the Army of Northern Virginia!

When large bodies of troops were moving on the same road, the alternate "halt" and "forward" was very harassing. Every obstacle produced a halt, and caused the men at once to sit and lie down on the roadside where shade or grass tempted them; about the time they got fixed they would hear the word "forward!" and then have to move at increased speed to close up the gap in the column. Sitting down for a few minutes on a long march is pleasant, but it does not always pay; when the march is resumed the limbs are stiff and sore, and the man rather worsted by the halt.

About noon on a hot day, some fellow with the water instinct would determine in his own mind that a well was not far ahead, and start off in a trot to reach it before the column. Of course another and another followed, till a stream of men were hurrying to the well, which was soon completely surrounded by a thirsty

mob, yelling and pushing and pulling to get to
the bucket as the windlass brought it again and
again to the surface.   But their impatience and
haste would soon overturn the windlass, and
spatter the water all around the well till the
whole crowd were wading in mud, the rope
would break, and the bucket fall to the bot-

A WELL

tom.   But there was a substitute for rope and
bucket.   The men would hasten away and get
long, slim poles, and on them tie, by the straps
a number of canteens, which they lowered
into the well and filled; and unless, as was frequently the case, the whole lot slipped off and
fell to the bottom, drew them to the top and
distributed them to their owners, who at once

threw their heads back, inserted the nozzles in their mouths and drank the last drop, hastening at once to rejoin the marching column, leaving behind them a dismantled and dry well. It was in vain that the officers tried to stop the stream of men making for the water, and equally vain to attempt to move the crowd while a drop remained accessible. Many, who were thoughtful, carried full canteens to comrades in the column, who had not been able to get to the well; and no one who has not had experience of it knows the thrill of gratification and delight which those fellows felt when the cool stream gurgled from the battered canteen down their parched throats.

In very hot weather, when the necessities of the service permitted, there was a halt about noon, of an hour or so, to rest the men and give them a chance to cool off and get the sand and gravel out of their shoes. This time was spent by some in absolute repose; but the lively boys told many a yarn, cracked many a joke, and sung many a song between " Halt " and " Column forward! " Some took the opportunity, if water was near, to bathe their feet, hands, and face, and nothing could be more enjoyable.

The passage of a cider cart (a barrel on wheels) was a rare and exciting occurrence.

4

The rapidity with which a barrel of sweet cider was consumed would astonish any one who saw it for the first time, and generally the owner had cause to wonder at the small return in cash. Sometimes a desperately enterprising darkey would approach the column with a cartload of pies, "so-called." It would be impossible to describe accurately the taste or appearance of those pies. They were generally similar in appearance, size, and thickness to a pale specimen of "Old Virginia" buckwheat cakes, and had a taste which resembled a combination of rancid lard and crab apples. It was generally supposed that they contained dried apples, and the sellers were careful to state that they had "sugar in 'em" and were "mighty nice." It was rarely the case that any "trace" of sugar was found, but they filled up a hungry man wonderfully.

Men of sense, and there were many such in the ranks, were necessarily desirous of knowing where or how far they were to march, and suffered greatly from a feeling of helpless ignorance of where they were and whither bound — whether to battle or camp. Frequently, when anticipating the quiet and rest of an ideal camp, they were thrown, weary and exhausted, into the face of a waiting enemy, and at times, after anticipating a sharp fight, having formed line

of battle and braced themselves for the coming
danger, suffered all the apprehension and got
themselves in good fighting trim, they were
marched off in the driest and prosiest sort of
style and ordered into camp, where, in all probability, they had to "wait for the wagon,"
and for the bread and meat therein, until the
proverb, " Patient waiting is no loss," lost all
its force and beauty.

Occasionally, when the column extended for
a mile or more, and the road was one dense
moving mass of men, a cheer would be heard
away ahead, — increasing in volume as it approached, until there was one universal shout.
Then some favorite general officer, dashing by,
followed by his staff, would explain the cause.
At other times, the same cheering and enthusiasm would result from the passage down the column of some obscure and despised officer, who
knew it was all a joke, and looked mean and
sheepish accordingly. But no *man* could produce more prolonged or hearty cheers than the
" old hare " which jumped the fence and invited
the column to a chase ; and often it was said,
when the rolling shout arose : " There goes old
General Lee or a Molly Cotton Tail ! "

The men would help each other when in real
distress, but their delight was to torment any
one who was unfortunate in a ridiculous way.

If, for instance, a piece of artillery was fast in the mud, the infantry and cavalry passing around the obstruction would rack their brains for words and phrases applicable to the situation, and most calculated to worry the cannoniers, who, waist deep in the mud, were tugging at the wheels.

Brass bands, at first quite numerous and good, became very rare and their music very poor in the latter years of the war. It was a fine thing to see the fellows trying to keep the music going as they waded through the mud. But poor as the music was, it helped the footsore and weary to make another mile, and encouraged a cheer and a brisker step from the lagging and tired column.

As the men tired, there was less and less talking, until the whole mass became quiet and serious. Each man was occupied with his own thoughts. For miles nothing could be heard but the steady tramp of the men, the rattling and jingling of canteens and accoutrements, and the occasional " Close up, men, — close up! " of the officers.

The most refreshing incidents of the march occurred when the column entered some clean and cosy village where the people loved the troops. Matron and maid vied with each other in their efforts to express their devotion to the

defenders of their cause. Remembering with
tearful eyes the absent soldier brother or husband, they yet smiled through their tears, and
with hearts and voices welcomed the coming
of the road-stained troops. Their scanty lard-
ers poured out the last morsel, and their bravest words were spoken, as the column moved
by. But who will tell the bitterness of the
lot of the man who thus passed by his own
sweet home, or the anguish of the mother as
she renewed her farewell to her darling boy?
Then it was that men and women learned to
long for the country where partings are no
more.

As evening came on, questioning of the officers was in order, and for an hour it would be,
"Captain, when are we going into camp?" "I
say, lieutenant, are we going to —— or to
——?" "Seen anything of our wagon?"
"How long are we to stay here?" "Where's
the spring?" Sometimes these questions were
meant simply to tease, but generally they be-
trayed anxiety of some sort, and a close ob-
server would easily detect the seriousness of the
man who asked after " our wagon," because he
spoke feelingly, as one who wanted his supper
and was in doubt as to whether or not he would
get it. People who live on country roads rarely
know how far it is from anywhere to any-

where else. This is a distinguishing peculiarity of that class of people. If they do know, then they are a malicious crew. " Just over the hill there," " Just beyond those woods," " 'Bout a mile," " Round the bend," and other such encouraging replies, mean anything from a mile to a day's march !

An accomplished straggler could assume more misery, look more horribly emaciated, tell more dismal stories of distress, eat more and march further (to the rear), than any ten ordinary men. Most stragglers were real sufferers, but many of them were ingenious liars, energetic foragers, plunder hunters and gormandizers. Thousands who kept their place in ranks to the very end were equally as tired, as sick, as hungry, and as hopeless, as these scamps, but too proud to tell it or use it as a means of escape from hardship. But many a poor fellow dropped in the road and breathed his last in the corner of a fence, with no one to hear his last fond mention of his loved ones. And many whose ambition it was to share every danger and discomfort with their comrades, overcome by the heat, or worn out with disease, were compelled to leave the ranks, and while friend and brother marched to battle, drag their weak and staggering frames to the rear, perhaps to die pitiably alone, in some hospital.

AN ACCOMPLISHED STRAGGLER.

After all, the march had more pleasure than pain. Chosen friends walked and talked and smoked together; the hills and valleys made themselves a panorama for the feasting of the soldiers' eyes; a turnip patch here and an onion patch there invited him to occasional refreshment; and it was sweet to think that "camp" was near at hand, and rest, and the journey almost ended.

CHAPTER V.

COOKING AND EATING.

RATIONS in the Army of Northern Virginia
were alternately superabundant and altogether
wanting. The quality, quantity, and frequency
of them depended upon the amount of stores in
the hands of the commissaries, the relative position of the troops and the wagon trains, and
the many accidents and mishaps of the campaign. During the latter years and months of
the war, so uncertain was the issue as to time,
quantity, and composition, that the men became
in large measure independent of this seeming absolute necessity, and by some mysterious means,
known only to purely patriotic soldiers, learned
to fight without pay and to find subsistence in
the field, the stream, or the forest, and a shelter
on the bleak mountain side.

Sometimes there was an abundant issue of
bread, and no meat; then meat in any quantity,
and no flour or meal; sugar in abundance, and
no coffee to be had for " love or money ; " and
then coffee in plenty, without a grain of sugar ;
for months nothing but flour for bread, and

THE COOK'S PREROGATIVES INVADED.

then nothing but meal (till all hands longed for a biscuit); or fresh meat until it was nauseating, and then salt-pork without intermission.

To be one day without anything to eat was common. Two days' fasting, marching and fighting was not uncommon, and there were times when no rations were issued for three or four days. On one march, from Petersburg to Appomattox, no rations were issued to Cutshaw's battalion of artillery for one entire week, and the men subsisted on the corn intended for the battery horses, raw bacon captured from the enemy, and the water of springs, creeks, and rivers.

A soldier in the Army of Northern Virginia was fortunate when he had his flour, meat, sugar, and coffee all at the same time and in proper quantity. Having these, the most skillful axeman of the mess hewed down a fine hickory or oak, and cut it into "lengths." All hands helped to "tote" it to the fire. When wood was convenient, the fire was large, the red coals abundant, and the meal soon prepared.

The man most gifted in the use of the skillet was the one most highly appreciated about the fire, and as tyrannical as a Turk; but when he raised the lid of the oven and exposed the brown-crusted tops of the biscuit, animosity sub-

sided.   The frying-pan, full of "grease," then
became the centre of attraction.   As the hol-
low-cheeked boy "sopped" his biscuit, his poor,
pinched countenance wrinkled into a smile, and
his sunken eyes glistened with delight.   And
the coffee, too, — how delicious the aroma of it,
and how readily each man disposed of a quart!
The strong men gathered round, chuckling at
their good luck, and "cooing" like a child with
a big piece of cake.   Ah, this was a sight which
but few of those who live and die are permitted
to see !

And now the last biscuit is gone, the last
drop of coffee, and the frying-pan is "wiped"
clean.   The tobacco-bag is pulled wide open,
pipes are scraped, knocked out, and filled, the
red coal is applied, and the blue smoke rises in
wreaths and curls from the mouths of the no
longer hungry, but happy and contented soldiers.   Songs rise on the still night air, the
merry laugh resounds, the woods are bright
with the rising flame of the fire, story after
story is told, song after song is sung, and at
midnight the soldiers steal away one by one to
their blankets on the ground, and sleep till re-
veillé.   Such was a meal when the mess was
fortunate.

How different when the wagons have not been
heard from for forty-eight hours.   Now the ques-

tion is, how to do the largest amount of good to the largest number with the smallest amount of material? The most experienced men discuss the situation and decide that " somebody " must go foraging. Though the stock on hand is small, no one seems anxious to leave the small certainty and go in search of the large uncertainty of supper from some farmer's well-filled table; but at last several comrades start out, and as they disappear the preparations for immediate consumption commence. The meat is too little to cook alone, and the flour will scarcely make six biscuits. The result is that " slosh " or " coosh " must do. So the bacon is fried out till the pan is half full of boiling grease. The flour is mixed with water until it flows like milk, poured into the grease and rapidly stirred till the whole is a dirty brown mixture. It is now ready to be served. Perhaps some dainty fellow prefers the more imposing " slapjack." If so, the flour is mixed with less water, the grease reduced, and the paste poured in till it covers the bottom of the pan, and, when brown on the underside, is, by a nimble twist of the pan, turned and browned again. If there is any sugar in camp it makes a delicious addition.

About the time the last scrap of " slapjack " and the last spoonful of " slosh " are disposed

of, the unhappy foragers return.   They take in
the situation at a glance, realize with painful
distinctness that they have sacrificed the homely
slosh for the vain expectancy of apple butter,
shortcake, and milk, and, with woeful countenance and mournful voice, narrate their adven-
ture and disappointment thus : " Well, boys, we
have done the best we could.   We have walked
about nine miles over the mountain, and have n't
found a mouthful to eat.   Sorry, but it 's a fact.
Give us our biscuits."   Of course there are none,
and, as it is not contrary to army etiquette to
do so, the whole mess professes to be very
sorry.   Sometimes, however, the foragers returned well laden with good things, and as
good comrades should, shared the fruits of their
toilsome hunt with their comrades.

Foragers thought it not indelicate to linger
about the house of the unsuspecting farmer till
the lamp revealed the family at supper, and
then modestly approach and knock at the door.
As the good-hearted man knew that his guests
were "posted " about the meal in progress in
the next room, the invitation to supper was
given, and, shall I say it, accepted with an un-
becoming lack of reluctance.

The following illustrates the ingenuity of the
average forager.   There was great scarcity of
meat, and no prospect of a supply from the wag-

ons. Two experienced foragers were sent out,
and as a farmer about ten miles from the camp
was killing hogs, guided by soldier instinct,
they went directly to his house, and found the
meat nicely cut up, the various pieces of each
hog making a separate pile on the floor of an
outhouse. The proposition to buy met with a
surprisingly ready response on the part of the
farmer. He offered one entire pile of meat, being one whole hog, for such a small sum that
the foragers instantly closed the bargain, and as
promptly opened their eyes to the danger which
menaced them. They gave the old gentleman
a ten-dollar bill and requested change. Pleased
with their honest method he hastened away
to his house to obtain it. The two honest
foragers hastily examined the particular pile
of pork which the simple-hearted farmer desig-
nated as theirs, found it very rank and totally
unfit for food, transferred half of it to another
pile, from which they took half and added to
theirs, and awaited the return of the farmer.
On giving them their change, he assured them
that they had a bargain. They agreed that
they had, tossed good and bad together in a
bag, said good-by, and departed as rapidly as
artillerymen on foot can. The result of the trip
was a "pot-pie" of large dimensions; and some
six or eight men gorged with fat pork declared

that they had never cared for and would not again wish to eat pork, — especially pork-pies.

A large proportion of the eating of the army was done in the houses and at the tables of the people, not by the use of force, but by the wish and invitation of the people. It was at times necessary that whole towns should help to sustain the army of defense, and when this was the case, it was done voluntarily and cheerfully. The soldiers — all who conducted themselves properly — were received as honored guests and given the best in the house. There was a wonderful absence of stealing or plundering, and even when the people suffered from depredation they attributed the cause to terrible necessity rather than to wanton disregard of the rights of property. And when armed guards were placed over the smoke-houses and barns, it was not so much because the commanding general doubted the honesty as that he knew the necessities of his troops. But even pinching hunger was not held to be an excuse for marauding expeditions.

The inability of the government to furnish supplies forced the men to depend largely upon their own energy and ingenuity to obtain them. The officers, knowing this, relaxed discipline to an extent which would seem, to a European officer, for instance, ruinous.· It was no uncommon sight to see a brigade or division, which was but a moment before marching in solid column along the road, scattered over an immense field searching for the luscious blackberries. And it was wonderful to see how promptly and cheerfully all returned to the ranks when the field was gleaned. In the fall of the year a persimmon tree on the roadside would halt a column and detain it till the last persimmon disappeared.

The sutler's wagon, loaded with luxuries, which was so common in the Federal army, was unknown in the Army of Northern Virginia, for two reasons: the men had no money to buy sutlers' stores, and the country no men to spare for sutlers. The nearest approach to the sutler's wagon was the "cider cart" of some old darkey, or a basket of pies and cakes displayed on the roadside for sale.

The Confederate soldier relied greatly upon the abundant supplies of eatables which the enemy was kind enough to bring him, and he cheerfully risked his life for the accomplishment of the twofold purpose of whipping the enemy and getting what he called "a square meal." After a battle there was general feasting on the Confederate side. Good things, scarcely ever seen at other times, filled the haversacks and the stomachs of the "Boys in Gray." Imagine the feelings of men half famished when they rush into a camp at one side, while the enemy flees from the other, and find the coffee on the fire, sugar at hand ready to be dropped into the coffee, bread in the oven, crackers by the box, fine beef ready cooked, desiccated vegetables by the bushel, canned peaches, lobsters, tomatoes, milk, barrels of ground and roasted coffee, soda, salt, and in short everything a hungry soldier craves. Then add the liquors, wines, cigars, and tobacco found in the tents of the officers and the wagons of the sutlers, and, remembering the condition of the victorious party, hungry, thirsty, and weary, say if it did not require wonderful devotion to duty, and great self-denial to push on, trampling under foot the plunder of the camp, and pursue the enemy till the sun went down.

When it was allowable to halt, what a glorious time it was! Men, who a moment before would have been delighted with a pone of corn-bread and a piece of fat meat, discuss the comparative merits of peaches and milk and fresh tomatoes, lobster and roast beef, and, forgetting the briar-root pipe, faithful companion of the vicissitudes of the soldier's life, snuff the aroma of imported Havanas.

In sharp contrast with the mess-cooking at the big fire was the serious and diligent work of the man separated from his comrades, out of reach of the woods, but bent on cooking and eating. He has found a coal of fire, and having placed over it, in an ingenious manner, the few leaves and twigs near his post, he fans the little pile with his hat. It soon blazes. Fearing the utter consumption of his fuel, he hastens to balance on the little fire his tin cup of water. When it boils, from some secure place in his clothes he takes a little coffee and drops it in the cup, and almost instantly the cup is removed and set aside; then a slice of fat meat is laid on the coals, and when brown and crisp, completes the meal — for the " crackers," or biscuit, are ready. No one but a soldier would have undertaken to cook with such a fire, as frequently it was no bigger than a quart cup.

Crackers, or " hard tack " as they were called, are notoriously poor eating, but in the hands of the Confederate soldier were made to do good duty. When on the march and pressed for time, a piece of solid fat pork and a dry cracker was passable or luscious, as the time was long or short since the last meal. When there was leisure to do it, hardtack was soaked well and then fried in bacon grease. Prepared thus, it was a dish which no Confederate had the weakness or the strength to refuse.

Sorghum, in the absence of the better molasses of peace times, was greatly prized and

5

eagerly sought after. A " Union " man living near the Confederate lines was one day busy boiling his crop. Naturally enough, some of " our boys " smelt out the place and determined to have some of the sweet fluid. They had found a yearling dead in the field hard by, and in thinking over the matter determined to sell the Union man if possible. So they cut from the dead animal a choice piece of beef, carried it to the old fellow and offered to trade. He accepted the offer, and the whole party walked off with canteens full.

Artillerymen, having tender consciences and no muskets, seldom, if ever, shot stray pigs; but they did sometimes, as an act of friendship, wholly disinterested, point out to the infantry a pig which seemed to need shooting, and by way of dividing the danger and responsibility of the act, accept privately a choice part of the deceased.

On one occasion, when a civilian was dining with the mess, there was a fine pig for dinner. This circumstance caused the civilian to re- mark on the good fare. The " forager " replied that pig was an uncommon dish, this one having been kicked by one of the battery horses while stealing corn, and instantly killed. The civilian seemed to doubt the statement after his teeth had come down hard on a pistol bullet, and continued to doubt, though assured that it was the head of a horse-shoe nail.

The most melancholy eating a soldier was ever forced to do, was, when pinched with hunger, cold, wet, and dejected, he wandered over the deserted field of battle and satisfied his cravings with the contents of the haversacks of the dead. If there is anything which will overcome the natural abhorrence which a man feels for the enemy, the loathing of the bloated dead, and the awe engendered by the presence of death, solitude, and silence, it is hunger. Impelled by its clamoring, men of high principle and tenderest humanity become for the time void of sensibility, and condescend to acts which, though justified by their extremity, seem afterwards, even to the doers, too shameless to mention.

When rations became so very small that it was absolutely necessary to supplement them, and the camp was permanently established, those men who had the physical ability worked for the neighborhood farmers at cutting cord-wood, harvesting the crops, killing hogs, or any other farm-work. A stout man would cut a cord of wood a day and receive fifty cents in money, or its equivalent in something eatable. Hogs were slaughtered for the "fifth quarter." When the corn became large enough to eat, the roasting ears, thrown in the ashes with the shucks on, and nicely roasted, made a grateful meal. Turnip and onion patches also furnished delightful and much-needed food, good raw or cooked.

Occasionally, when a mess was hard pushed for eatables, it became necessary to resort to some ingenious method of disgusting a part of the mess, that the others might eat their fill. The "pepper treatment" was a common method practiced with the soup, which once failed. A shrewd fellow, who loved things "hot," decided to have plenty of soup, and to accomplish his purpose, as he passed and repassed the boiling pot, dropped in a pod of red pepper. But, alas! for him, there was another man like minded who adopted the same plan, and the result was that all the mess waited in vain for that pot of soup to cool.

The individual coffee-boiler of one man in the Army of Northern Virginia was always kept at the boiling point. The owner of it was an enigma to his comrades. They could not understand his strange fondness for "red-hot" coffee. Since the war he has explained that he found the heat of the coffee prevented its use by others, and adopted the plan of placing his cup on the fire after every sip. This same character never troubled himself to carry a canteen, though a great water drinker. When he found a good canteen he would kindly give it to a comrade, reserving the privilege of an occasional drink when in need. He soon had an interest in thirty or forty canteens and their contents, and could always get a drink of water if it was to be found in any of them. He pursued the same plan with blankets, and always had plenty in that line. His entire outfit was the clothes on his back and a haversack accurately shaped to hold one half pone of corn bread.

Roasting-ear time was a trying time for the hungry private. Having been fed during the whole of the winter on salt meat and coarse bread, his system craved the fresh, luscious juice of the corn, and at times his honesty gave way under the pressure. How could he resist? He did n't, — he took some roasting ears! Sometimes the farmer grumbled, sometimes he quarreled, and sometimes he complained to the officers of the depredations of "the men." The officers apologized, ate what corn they had on hand, and sent their "boy" for some more. One old farmer conceived the happy plan of inviting some privates to his house, stating his grievances, and securing their coöperation in the effort to protect his corn. He told them that of course *they* were not the *gentlemen* who took his corn! Oh no! of course *they* would not do such a thing; but would n't they please speak to the others and ask them please not to take his corn? Of course! certainly! oh, yes! they would remonstrate with their comrades. How they burned, though, as they thought of the past and contemplated the near future. As they returned to camp through the field they filled their haversacks with the silky ears, and were met on the other side of the field by the kind farmer and a file of men, who were only too eager to secure the plucked corn "in the line of duty."

A faithful officer, worn out with the long, weary march, sick, hungry, and dejected, leaned his back against a tree and groaned to think of his inability to join in the chase of an old hare, which, he knew, from the wild yells in the wood, his men were pursuing. But the uproar approached him — nearer, nearer, and nearer, until he saw the hare bounding towards him with a regiment at her heels. She spied an opening made by the folds of the officer's cloak and jumped in, and he embraced his first meal for forty-eight hours.

An artilleryman, camped for a day where no water was to be found easily, awakened during the night by thirst, went stumbling about in search of water; and to his great delight found a large bucketful. He drank his fill, and in the morning found that what he drank had washed a bullock's head, and was crimson with its blood.

Some stragglers came up one night and found the camp silent. All hands asleep. Being hungry they sought and to their great delight found a large pot of soup. It had a peculiar taste, but they " worried " it down, and in the morning bragged of their good fortune. The soup had defied the stomachs of the whole battery, being strongly impregnated with the peculiar flavor of defunct cockroaches.

Shortly before the evacuation of Petersburg, a country boy went hunting. He killed and brought to camp a muskrat. It was skinned, cleaned, buried a day or two, disinterred, cooked, and eaten with great relish. It was splendid.

During the seven days' battles around Richmond, a studious private observed the rats as they entered and emerged from a corn-crib. He killed one, cooked it privately, and invited a friend to join him in eating a fine squirrel. The comrade consented, ate heartily, and when told what he had eaten, forthwith disgorged. But he confesses that up to the time when he was enlightened he had greatly enjoyed the meal.

It was at this time, when rats were a delicacy, that the troops around Richmond agreed to divide their rations with the poor of the city, and they were actually hauled in and distributed. Comment here would be like complimenting the sun on its brilliancy.

Orators dwell on the genius and skill of the general officers; historians tell of the movements of divisions and army corps, and the student of the art of war studies the geography and topography of the country and the returns of the various corps: they all seek to find and to tell the secret of success or failure. The Confederate soldier knows the elements of his success — courage, endurance, and devotion. He knows also by whom he was defeated — sickness, starvation, death. He fought not men only, but food, raiment, pay, glory, fame, and fanaticism. He endured privation, toil, and contempt. He won, and despite the cold indifference of all and the hearty hatred of some, he will have for all time, in all places where generosity is, a fame untarnished.

CHAPTER VI.

COMFORTS, CONVENIENCES, AND CONSOLATIONS.

HAVE you ever been a soldier ? No ? Then you do not know what comforts are! Conveniences you never had; animal consolations, never! You have not enjoyed the great exceptional luxuries which once in a century, perhaps, bless a limited number of men. How sad, that you have allowed your opportunity to pass unimproved !

But you *have* been a soldier! Ah, then let us together recall with pleasure, the past! once more be hungry, and eat ; once more tired, and rest ; once more thirsty, and drink ; once more, cold and wet, let us sit by the roaring fire and feel comfort creep over us. So ! — isn't it very pleasant ?

Now let us recount, repossess rather, the treasures which once were ours, not forgetting that values have shrunk, and that the times have changed, and that men also are changed ; some happily, some wofully. Possibly we, also, are somewhat modified.

Eating, you will remember, was more than a convenience; it was a comfort which rose almost to the height of a consolation. Probably the most universally desired comfort of the Confederate soldier was "something to eat." But this, like all greatly desired blessings, was shy, and when obtained was, to the average seeker, not replete with satisfaction.

But he did eat, at times, with great energy, great endurance, great capacity, and great satisfaction ; the luscious slapjack, sweetened perhaps with sorghum, the yellow and odoriferous soda-biscuit, ash-cake, or, it might chance to be, the faithful "hardtack" (which "our friends the enemy" called "crackers") serving in rotation as bread.

The faithful hog was everywhere represented. His cheering presence was manifested most agreeably by the sweet odors flung to the breeze from the frying-pan, — that never failing and always reliable utensil. The solid slices of streaked lean and fat, the limpid gravy, the brown pan of slosh inviting you to sop it, and the rare, delicate shortness of the biscuit, made the homely animal to be in high esteem.

Beef, glorious beef! how seldom were you seen, and how welcome was your presence. In the generous pot you parted with your mysterious strength and sweetness. Impaled upon the cruel ramrod you suffered slow torture over the fire. Sliced, chopped, and pounded; boiled, stewed, fried, or broiled, always a trusty friend, and sweet comforter.

Happy the "fire" where the "stray" pig found a lover, and unhappy the pig! Innocence and youth were no protection to him, and his cries of distress availed him not as against the cruel purpose of the rude soldiery.

What is that faint aroma which steals about on the night air? Is it a celestial breeze? No! it is the mist of the coffee-boiler. Do you not hear the tumult of the tumbling water? Poor man! you have eaten, and now other joys press upon you. Drink! drink more! Near the bottom it is sweeter. Providence hath now joined together for you the bitter and the sweet, — there is sugar in that cup!

Some poor fellows, after eating, could only sleep. They were incapable of the noble satisfaction of "a good smoke." But there were some good men and true, thoughtful men, quietly disposed men, gentle and kind, who, next to a good "square" meal prized a smoke. Possibly, here begins consolation. Who can find words to tell the story of the soldier's affection for his faithful briar-root pipe! As the cloudy incense of the weed rises in circling wreaths about his head, as he hears the mur-

muring of the fire, and watches the glowing and fading of the embers, and feels the comfort of the hour pervading his mortal frame, what bliss!

But yonder sits a man who scorns the pipe — and why? He is a chewer of the weed. To him, the sweetness of it seems not to be drawn out by the fiery test, but rather by the persuasion of moisture and pressure. But he, too, is under the spell. There are pictures in the fire for him, also, and he watches them come and go. Now draw near. Are not those cheerful voices? Do you not hear the contented tones of men sitting in a cosy home? What glowing hopes here leap out in rapid words! No bitterness of hate, no revenge, no cruel purpose; but simply the firm resolve to march in the front of their country's defenders. Would you hear a song? You shall, — for even now they sing:

> " Aha! a song for the trumpet's tongue!
> For the bugle to sing before us,
> When our gleaming guns, like clarions,
> Shall thunder in battle chorus! "

Would you hear a soldier's prayer? Well, there kneels one, behind that tree, but he talks with God: you may not hear him — nor I!

But now, there they go, one by one; no, two by two. Down goes an old rubber blanket, and then a good, thick, woolen one, probably with a big " U. S." in the centre of it. Down go two men. They are hidden under another of the " U. S." blankets. They are resting their heads on their old battered haversacks. They love each other to the death, those men, and sleep there, like little children, locked in close embrace. They are asleep now, — no, not quite ; they are thinking of home, and it may be, of heaven. But now, surely they are asleep ! No, they are not quite asleep, they are falling off to sleep. Happy soldiers, they are asleep.

At early dawn the bugle sounds the reveille. Shout answers to shout, the roll is called and the day begins. What new joys will it bring ? Let us stay and see.

The sun gladdens the landscape ; the fresh air, dashing and whirling over the fields and through the pines is almost intoxicating. Here are noble chestnut-oaks, ready for the axe and the fire ; and there, at the foot of the hill, a mossy spring. The oven sits enthroned on glowing coals, crowned with fire ; the coffee boils, the meat fries, the soldier — smiles and waits.

But waiting is so very trying that some, seizing towels, soap, and comb from their haversacks, step briskly down the hill, and plunge their heads into the cool water of the brook.

Then their cheeks glow with rich color, and, chatting merrily, they seek again the fire, carrying the old bucket brimming full of water for the mess. All hands welcome the bucket, and breakfast begins. Now see the value of a good tin-plate. What a treasure that tin cup is, and that old fork! Who would have a more comfortable seat than that log affords!

But here comes the mail, — papers, letters, packages. Here comes news from home, sweet, tender, tearful, hopeful, sad, distressing news; joyful news of victory and sad news of defeat; pictures of happy homes, or sad wailing over homes destroyed! But the mail has arrived and we cannot change the burden it has brought. We can only pity the man who goes empty away from the little group assembled about the mail-bag, and rejoice with him who strolls away with a letter near his heart. Suppose he finds therein the picture of a curly head. Just four years old! Suppose the last word in it is "Mother." Or suppose it concludes with a signature having that peculiarly helpless, but courageous and hopeful air, which can be imparted only by the hand of a girl whose heart goes with the letter! Once more, happy, happy soldier!

The artilleryman tarrying for a day only in a camp had only time to eat and do his work.

Roll-call, drill, watering the horses, greasing caissons and gun-carriages; cleaning, repairing, and greasing harness; cleaning the chests of the limbers and caissons; storing and arranging ammunition; and many little duties, filled the day. In the midst of a campaign, comfortable arrangements for staying were hardly completed by the time the bugle sounded the assembly and orders to move were given. But however short the stay might be, the departure always partook of the nature of a move from home. More especially was this true in the case of the sick man, whose weary body was finding needed rest in the camp; and peculiarly true of the man who had fed at the table of a hospitable neighbor, and for a day, perhaps, enjoyed the society of the fair daughters of the house.

Orders to move were frequently heralded by the presence of the " courier," a man who rarely knew a word of the orders he had brought; who was always besieged with innumerable questions, always tried to appear to know more than his position allowed him to disclose, and who never ceased to be an object of interest to every camp he entered. Many a gallant fellow rode the country over; many a one led in the thickest of the fight and died bravely, known only as " my courier."

When the leaves began to fall and the wind

to rush in furious frolics through the woods, the soldier's heart yearned for comfort. Chilling rains, cutting sleet, drifting snow, muddy roads, all the miseries of approaching winter, pressed him to ask and repeat the question, "When will we go into winter quarters?"

After all, the time did come. But first the place was known. The time was always doubtful. Leisurely and steady movement towards the place might be called the first "comfort" of winter quarters; and as each day's march brought the column nearer the appointed camp, the anticipated pleasures assumed almost the sweetness of present enjoyment.

But at last comes the welcome "Left into park!" and the fence goes down, the first piece wheels through the gap, the battery is parked, the horses are turned over to the "horse sergeant," the old guns are snugly stowed under the tarpaulins, and the winter has commenced. The woods soon resound with the ring of the axe; trees rush down, crashing and snapping, to the ground; fires start here and there till the woods are illuminated, and the brightest, happiest, busiest night of all the year falls upon the camp. Now around each fire gathers the little group who are, for a while, to make it the centre of operations. Hasty plans for comfort and convenience are eagerly discussed till late into the night, and await only the dawn of another day for execution.

Roll-call over and breakfast eaten, the work of the day commences with the preparation of comfortable sleeping places, varying according to the "material" on hand. A favorite arrangement for two men consisted of a bed of clean straw between the halves of a large oak log, covered, in the event of rain, with a rubber blanket. The more ambitious builders made straw pens, several logs high, and pitched over these a fly-tent, adding sometimes a chimney. In this structure, by the aid of a bountiful supply of dry, clean straw, and their blankets, the occupants bade defiance to cold, rain, and snow.

Other men, gifted with that strange facility for comfort without work which characterizes some people, found resting-places ready made. They managed to steal away night after night and sleep in the sweet security of a haystack, a barn, a stable, a porch, or, if fortune favored them, in some farmer's feather bed.

Others still, but more especially the infantry and cavalry, built "shelters" open to the south, covered them with pine-tags and brush, built a huge fire in front, and made themselves at home for a season.

But all these things were mere make-shifts, temporary stopping-places, occupying about the

6

same relation to winter quarters as the board-ing-house does to a happy and comfortable home. During the occupancy of these, and while the work of building was progressing, the Confed-erate soldier wrote many letters home. He saw an opportunity for enjoyment ahead, and tried to improve it. His letters were somewhat after the following order: —

CAMP NEAR WILLIAMS' MILL,
December 2, 1864.

DEAR FATHER, — You will no doubt be glad to hear that we are at last in winter quarters! We are quite comfortably fixed, though we arrived here only two days ago. We are working constantly on our log cabins, and hope to be in them next week. We are near the —— railroad, and anything you may desire to send us may be shipped to —— depot. If you can possibly spare the money to buy them, please send at once four pounds ten-penny nails; one pair wrought hinges (for door); one good axe; two pairs shoes (one for me and one for J.); four pairs socks (two for me and two for J.); five pounds Killickinick smoking tobacco; one pound bi-carb. soda. Please send also two or three old church music books, and any good books you are willing to part with forever. Underclothing of any sort, shirts, drawers, socks, — cotton or woollen, — would be very, very acceptable, as it is much less trouble to put on the clean and throw away the soiled clothes than to wash them. Some coffee, roasted and ground, with sugar to match, and *anything good to eat* would do to fill up. Do not imagine, however, that we are suffering or unhappy. Our only concern is for all at home; and if compliance with the above requests would cost you the slightest self-denial at home, we would rather withdraw them.

Why don't —— and —— go into the army? They are old enough, hearty enough, able to provide themselves with every comfort, and ought to be here.

Many furloughs will be granted during the winter, and we may get home, some of us, before another month is past.

Love to mother, dear mother; and to sister, and tell them we are happy and contented. Write as soon as you can, and believe me, Your affectionate son,

—— —— ——.

P. S. Don't forget the tobacco.   **W.**

And now another night comes to the soldier, inviting him to nestle in clean straw, under dry blankets, and sleep. To-morrow he will lay the foundation of a village destined to live till the grass grows again. To-morrow he will be architect, builder, and proprietor of a cosy cabin in the woods. Let him sleep.

A pine wood of heavy original growth furnishes the ground and the timber. Each company is to have two rows of houses, with a street between, and each street is to end on the main road to the railroad depot. The width of the street is decided; it is staked off; each " mess " selects its site for a house, and the work commences.

The old pines fall rapidly under the energetic strokes of the axes, which glide into the hearts of the trees with a malicious and cruel willingness ; the logs are cut into lengths, notched and fitted one upon another, and the structure begins to rise. The builders stagger about here and there, under the weight of the huge logs, occasionally falling and rolling in the snow. They shout and whistle and sing, and are as merry as children at play.

At last the topmost log is rolled into place and the artistic work commences, — the "riving " of slabs. Short logs of oak are to be split into huge shingles for the roof, and tough and tedious work it is. But it is done; the roof is covered in, and the house is far enough advanced for occupancy.

Now the " bunks," which are simply broad shelves one above another, wide enough to accommodate two men " spoon fashion," are built. Merry parties sally forth to seek the straw stack of the genial farmer of the period, and, returning heavily laden with sweet clean straw, bestow it in the bunks. Here they rest for a night.

Next day the chimney, built like the house, of notched sticks or small logs, rises rapidly, till it reaches the apex of the roof and is crowned with a nail keg or flour barrel.

Next, a pit is dug deep enough to reach the clay; water is poured in and the clay well mixed, and the whole mess takes in hand the "daubing" of the "chinks." Every crack and crevice of house and chimney receives attention at the hands of the builders, and when the sun goes down the house is proof against the most searching winter wind.

Now the most skillful man contrives a door and swings it on its hinges; another makes a shelf for the old water bucket; a short bench or two appear, like magicians' work, before the fire, and the family is settled for the winter.

It would be a vain man indeed who thought himself able to describe the happy days and cozy nights of that camp. First among the luxuries of settled life was the opportunity to part forever with a suit of underwear which had been on constant duty for, possibly, three months, and put on the sweet clean clothes from home. They looked so pure, and the very smell of them was sweet.

Then there was the ever-present thought of a dry, warm, undisturbed sleep the whole night through. What a comfort!

Remember, now, there is a pile of splendid oak, ready cut for the fire, within easy reach of the door — several cords of it — and it is all ours. Our mess cut it and "toted" it there.

It will keep a good fire, night and day, for a month.

The wagons, which have been "over the mountains and far away," have come into camp loaded with the best flour in abundance; droves of cattle are bellowing in the road, and our commissary, as he hurries from camp to camp with the glad tidings, is the embodiment of happiness. All this means plenty to eat.

This is a good time to make and carve beautiful pipes of hard wood with horn mouth-pieces, very comfortable chairs, bread trays, haversacks, and a thousand other conveniences.

At night the visiting commences, and soon in many huts are little social groups close around the fire. The various incidents of the campaign pass in review, and pealing laughter rings out upon the crisp winter air. Then a soft, sweet melody floats out of that cabin door as the favorite singer yields to the entreaty of his little circle of friends; or a swelling chorus of manly voices, chanting a grand and solemn anthem, stirs every heart for half a mile around.

Now think of an old Confederate veteran, who passed through Fredericksburg, Chancellorsville, and the Wilderness, sitting in front of a cheerful fire in a snug log cabin, reading, say, "The Spectator!" Think of another by his side reading a letter from his sweetheart; and an-

AN INNOCENT VICTIM

other still, a warm and yearning letter from his mother. Think of two others in the corner playing "old sledge," or, it may be, chess. *Hear* another, "off guard," snoring in his bunk. Ah! what an amount of condensed contentment that little hut contains.

And now the stables are finished. The whole battalion did the work, and the poor old shivering and groaning horses are under cover. And the guard-house, another joint production, opens wide its door every day to receive the unhappy men whose time for detail has at last arrived. The chapel, an afterthought, is also ready for use, having been duly dedicated to the worship of God. The town is complete and its citizens are happy.

Men thus comfortably fixed, with light guard duty and little else to do, found time, of course, to do a little foraging in the country around. By this means often during the winter the camp enjoyed great abundance and variety of food. Apples and apple-butter, fresh pork, dried fruit, milk, eggs, risen bread, and even *cakes and preserves*. Occasionally a whole mess would be filled with the liveliest expectations by the information that "Bob" or "Joe" was expecting *a box from home*. The wagon comes into camp escorted by the expectant "Bob" and several of his intimate friends; the box is dropped from the wagon to the ground; off goes the top and in go busy hands and eyes. Here are clothes, shoes, and hats; here is coffee, sugar, soda, salt, bread, fresh butter, roast beef, and turkey; here is *a bottle!* marked "to be used in case of sickness or wounds." Here is paper, ink, pen and pencil. What shall be done with this pile of treasure? It is evident one man cannot eat the eatables or smoke the tobacco and pipes. Call in, then, the friendly aid of willing comrades. They come; they see; they devour!

And now the ever true and devoted citizens of the much and often besieged city of Richmond conclude to send a New Year's dinner to their defenders in the army. That portion destined for the camp above described arrived in due time in the shape of one good turkey. Each of the three companies composing the battalion appointed a man to "draw straws" for the turkey; the successful company appointed a man from each detachment to draw again; then the detachment messes took a draw, and the fortunate mess devoured the turkey. But the soldiers, remembering that in times past they had felt constrained to divide their rations with the poor of that city, did not fail in gratitude, or question the liberality of those who had, in the midst of great distress, remembered with self-denying affection the soldiers in the field.

Not the least among the comforts of life in winter quarters, was the pleasure of sitting under the ministrations of an amateur barber, and hearing the snip, snip, of his scissors, as the long growth of hair fell to the ground. The luxury of "a shave;" the possession of comb, brush, small mirror, towels and soap; boots blacked every day; white collars, and occasionally a starched bosom, called, in the expressive language of the day, a "*biled shirt*," completed the restoration of the man to decency. Now, also, the soldier with painful care threaded his needle with huge thread, and with a sort of left-handed awkwardness sewed on the long-absent button, or, with even greater trepidation, attempted a patch. At such a time the soldier pondered on the peculiar fact that war separates men from women. A man cannot thread a needle with ease; certainly not with grace. He sews backwards.

In winter quarters every man had his "chum" or bunk-mate, with whom he slept, walked, talked, and divided hardship or comfort as they came along; and the affectionate regard of each for the other was often beautiful to see. Many such attachments led to heroic self-denials and death, one for the other, and many such unions remain unbroken after twenty years have passed away.

It was a rare occurrence, but occasionally the father or mother or brother or sister of some man paid him a visit. The males were almost sure to be very old or very young. In either case they were received with great hospitality, given the best place to sleep, the best the camp afforded in the way of eatables, and treated with the greatest courtesy and kindness by the whole command. But the lady visitors! the girls! Who could describe the effect of their appearance in camp! They produced conflict in the soldier's breast. They looked so clean, they were so gentle, they were so different from all around them, they were so attractive, they were so agreeable, and sweet, and fresh, and happy, that the poor fellows would have liked above all things to have gotten very near to them and have heard their kind words, — possibly shake hands; but no, some were barefooted, some almost bareheaded; some were still expecting clean clothes from home; some were sick and disheartened; some were on guard; some *in the guard-house*, and others too modest; and so, to many, the innocent visitor became a sort of pleasant agony; as it were, a " bitter sweet." Nothing ever so promptly convinced a Confederate soldier that he was dilapidated and not altogether as neat as he might be, as sudden precipitation into the presence of a neatly dressed, refined, and modest woman. Fortunately for the men, the women loved the very rags they wore, if they were gray; and when the war ended, they welcomed with open arms and hearts full of love the man and his rags.

GIRLS
IN CAMP

Preaching in camp was to many a great pleasure and greatly profitable. At times intense religious interest pervaded the whole army, and thousands of men gladly heard the tidings of salvation. Many afterwards died triumphant, and many others are yet living, daily witnesses of the great change wrought in them by the preaching of the faithful and able men who, as chaplains, shared the dangers, hardships, and pleasures of the campaign.

To all the foregoing comforts and conven-

iences must be added the consolation afforded by
the anticipation and daily expectation of a furlough; which meant, of course, a blissful reunion with the dear ones at home, — perhaps
an interview or two with that historic maid who
is "left behind" by the soldier of all times
and lands; plenty to eat; general admiration
of friends and relatives; invitations to dine, to
spend a week; and last, but not least, an opportunity to express contempt for every able-
bodied "bomb-proof" found sneaking about
home. Food, shelter, and rest, the great con-
cerns, being thus all provided for, the soldier enjoyed intensely his freedom from care and responsibility, living, as near as a man may, the
innocent life of a child. He played marbles,
spun his top, played at foot-ball, bandy, and
hop-scotch; slept quietly, rose early, had a good
appetite, and was happy. He had time now
comfortably to review the toils, dangers, and
hardships of the past campaign, and with allowable pride to dwell on the cheerfulness and
courage with which he had endured them all;
and to feel the supporting effect of the unanim-
ity of feeling and pervasive sympathy which
linked together the rank and file of the army.

Leaving out of view every other consideration,
he realized with exquisite delight, that he was
resisting manfully the coercive force of other

men, and was resolved to die rather than yield his liberty. He felt that he was beyond doubt in the line of duty, and expected no relief from toil by any other means than the accomplishment of his purpose and the end of the war. To strengthen his resolve he had ever present with him the unchanging love of the people for whom he fought ; the respect and confidence of his officers ; unshaken faith in the valor of his comrades and the justice of his cause. And, finally, he had an opportunity to brace himself for another, and, if need be, for still another struggle, with the ever increasing multitude of invaders, hoping that each would usher in the peace so eagerly coveted and the liberty for which already a great price had been paid. Was he not badly disappointed ?

CHAPTER VII.

FUN AND FURY ON THE FIELD.

A BATTLE-FIELD, when only a few thousands of men are engaged, is a more extensive area than most persons would suppose. When large bodies of men — twenty to fifty thousand on each side — are engaged, a mounted man, at liberty to gallop from place to place, could scarcely travel the field over during the continuance of the battle; and a private soldier, in the smallest affair, sees very little indeed of the field. What occurs in his own regiment, or probably in his own company, is about all, and is sometimes more than he actually sees or knows. Thus it is that, while the field is extensive, it is to each individual limited to the narrow space of which he is cognizant.

The dense woods of Virginia, often choked with heavy undergrowth, added greatly to the difficulty of observing the movements of large bodies of troops extended in line of battle. The commanders were compelled to rely almost entirely upon the information gained from their staff officers and the couriers of those in immediate command on the lines.

The beasts of burden which travel the Great
Desert scent the oasis and the well miles away,
and, cheered by the prospect of rest and refreshment, press on with renewed vigor ; and in the
book of Job it is said of the horse, " He saith
among the trumpets, Ha! ha! and he smelleth
the battle afar off, the thunder of the captains,
and the shoutings." So a soldier, weary and
worn, recognizing the signs of approaching battle, did quicken his lagging steps and cry out
for joy at the prospect.

The column, hitherto moving forward with
the steadiness of a mighty river, hesitates,
halts, steps back, then forward, hesitates again,
halts. The colonels talk to the brigadier, the
brigadiers talk to the major-general, some officers hurry forward and others hurry to the rear.
Infantry stands to one side of the road while
cavalry trots by to the front. Now some old
wagons marked " Ord. Dept." go creaking and
rumbling by.   One or two light ambulances,
with a gay and careless air, seem to trip along
with the ease of a dancing-girl. They and the
surgeons seem cheerful. Some, not many,
ask " What is the matter?"   Most of the men
there know exactly : they are on the edge of
battle.

Presently a very quiet, almost sleepy looking
man on horseback, says, " Forward, 19th! " and

away goes the leading regiment.   A little way
ahead the regiment jumps a fence, and — pop !
bang ! whiz ! thud ! is all that can be heard,
until the rebel yell reverberates through the
woods.   Battle ?   No ! skirmishers advancing.

Step into the woods now and watch these
skirmishers.   See how cheerfully they go in.
How rapidly they load, fire, and re-load.   They
stand six and twelve feet apart, calling to each

GOING IN

other, laughing, shouting and cheering, but advancing.   There : one fellow has dropped his
musket like something red hot.   His finger is
shot away.   His friends congratulate him, and
he walks sadly away to the rear.   Another
staggers and falls with a ball through his neck,
mortally wounded.   Two comrades raise him to
his feet and try to lead him away, but one of
them receives a ball in his thigh which crushes
the bone, and he falls groaning to the ground.

The other advises his poor dying friend to lie down, helps him to do so, and runs to join his advancing comrades. When he overtakes them he finds every man securely posted behind a tree, loading, firing, and conducting himself generally with great deliberation and prudence. They have at last driven the enemy's skirmishers in upon the line of battle, and are waiting. A score of men have fallen here, some killed outright, some slightly, some sorely, and some mortally wounded. The elements now add to the horrors of the hour. Dense clouds hovering near the tree tops add deeper shadows to the woods. Thunder, deep and ominous, rolls in prolonged peals across the sky, and lurid lightning darts among the trees and glistens on the gun barrels. But still they stand.

Now a battery has been hurried into position, the heavy trails have fallen to the ground, and at the command "Commence firing!" the cannoniers have stepped in briskly and loaded. The first gun blazes at the muzzle and away goes a shell. The poor fellows in the woods rejoice as it crashes through the trees over their heads, and cheer when it explodes over the enemy's line. Now, what a chorus! Thunder, gun after gun, shell after shell, musketry, pelting rain, shouts, groans, cheers, and commands!

But help is coming. At the edge of the

7

woods, where the skirmishers entered, the brigade is in line. Somebody has ordered, " Load ! "

The ramrods glisten and rattle down the barrels of a thousand muskets. " F-o-o-o-o-r-r-r-r-w-a-a-a-r-r-r-d ! " is the next command, and the brigade disappears in the woods, the canteens rattling, the bushes crackling, and the officers never ceasing to say, " Close up, men ; close up ! guide c-e-n-t-r-r-r-r-e ! "

The men on that skirmish line have at last found it advisable to lie down at full length on the ground, though it is so wet, and place their heads against the trees in front. They cannot advance and they cannot retire without, in either case, exposing themselves to almost certain death. They are waiting for the line of battle to come to their relief.

At last, before they see, they hear the line advancing through the pines. The snapping of the twigs, the neighing of horses, and hoarse commands, inspire a husky cheer, and when the line of the old brigade breaks through the trees in full view, they fairly yell ! Every man jumps to his feet, the brigade presses firmly forward, and soon the roll of musketry tells all who are waiting to hear that serious work is progressing away down in the woods. All honor to the devoted infantry. The hour of glory has arrived for couriers, aides-de-camp,

EXTENDING THE REAR.

and staff officers generally. They dash about from place to place like spirits of unrest. Brigade after brigade and division after division is hurried into line, and pressed forward into action. Battalions of artillery open fire from the crests of many hills, and the battle is begun.

Ammunition trains climb impassable places, cross ditches without bridges, and manage somehow to place themselves in reach of the troops. Ambulances, which an hour before went gayly forward, now slowly and solemnly return loaded. Shells and musket balls which must have lost their way, go flitting about here and there, wounding and killing men who deem themselves far away from danger. The negro cooks turn pale as these unexpected visitors enter the camps at the rear, and the rear is " extended " at once.

But our place now is at the front, on the field. We are to watch the details of a small part of the great expanse. As we approach, a ludicrous scene presents itself. A strong-armed artilleryman is energetically thrashing a dejected looking individual with a hickory bush, and urging him to the front. He has managed to keep out of many a fight, but now he *must* go in. The captain has detailed a man to *whip* him in, and the man is doing it. With every blow the poor fellow yells and begs to be spared, but his determined guardian will not cease. They press on, the one screaming and the other lashing, till they reach the battery in position and firing on the retiring enemy. A battery of the enemy is replying, and shells are bursting overhead, or ploughing huge furrows in the ground. Musket balls are "rapping" on the rims of the wheels and sinking with a deep "thud" into the bodies of the poor horses. Smoke obscures the scene, but the cannoniers in faint outline can be seen cheerfully serving the guns.

As the opposing battery ceases firing, and having limbered up, scampers away, and the last of the enemy's infantry slowly sinks into the woods out of sight and out of reach, a wild cheer breaks from the cannoniers, who toss their caps in the air and shout, shake hands and shout again, while the curtain of smoke is raised by the breeze and borne away.

The cavalry is gone. With jingle and clatter they have passed through the lines and down the hill, and are already demanding surrender from many a belated man. There will be no rest for that retreating column. Stuart, with a twinkle in his eye, his lips puckered as if to whistle a merry lay, is on their flanks, in their rear, and in their front. The enemy will send their cavalry after him, of course, but he will stay with them, nevertheless.

Add now the stream of wounded men slowly
making their way to the rear; the groups of

dejected prisoners plodding along under guard,
and you have about as much of a battle as one
private soldier ever sees.

COMING OUT

But after the battle, man will tell to man

what each has seen and felt, until every man will feel that he has seen the whole. Hear, then, the stories of battle.

An artilleryman — he must have been a driver — says: when the firing had ceased an old battery horse, his lower jaw carried away by a shot, with blood streaming from his wound, staggered up to him, gazed beseechingly at him, and, groaning piteously, laid his bloody jaws on his shoulder, and so made his appeal for sympathy. He was beyond help.

The pathetic nature of this story reminds a comrade that a new man in the battery, desiring to save the labor incident to running up the gun after the rebound, determined to hold on to the handspike, press the trail into the ground, and hold her fast. He did try, but the rebound proceeded as usual, and the labor-saving man was "shocked" at the failure of his effort. Nothing daunted, the same individual soon after applied his lips to the vent of the gun, which was choked, and endeavored to clear it by an energetic blast from his lungs. The vent was not cleared but the lips of the recruit were nicely browned, and the detachment greatly amused.

At another gun it has happened that No. 1 and No. 3 have had a difficulty. No. 3 having failed to serve the vent, there was a premature explosion, and No. 1, being about to withdraw

the rammer, fell heavily to the ground, apparently dead. No. 3, seeing what a calamity he
had caused, hung over the dead man and begged
him to speak and exonerate him from blame.
After No. 3 had exhausted all his eloquence and
pathos, No. 1 suddenly rose to his feet and informed him that the premature explosion was
a fact, but the death of No. 1 was a joke intended to warn him that if he ever failed again
to serve that vent, he would have his head
broken by a blow from a rammer-head. This
joke having been completed in all its details,
the firing was continued.

Another man tells how Eggleston had his
arm torn away by a solid shot, and, as he walked
away, held up the bleeding, quivering stump,
exclaiming, " Never mind, boys ; I 'll come back
soon and try 'em with this other one." Alas!
poor fellow, he had fought his last fight.

Poor Tom, he who was always, as he said,
" willing to give 'em half a leg, or so," was
struck about the waist by a shot which almost
cut him in two. He fell heavily to the ground,
and, though in awful agony, managed to say :
" Tell mother I died doing my duty."

While the fight lasted, several of the best
and bravest received wounds apparently mortal,
and were laid aside covered by an old army blanket. They refused to die, however, and remain

to this day to tell their own stories of the war and of their marvelous recovery.

At the battle of the Wilderness, May, 1864, a man from North Carolina precipitated a severe fight by asking a very simple and reasonable question. The line of battle had been pressed forward and was in close proximity to the enemy. The thick and tangled undergrowth prevented a sight of the enemy, but every man felt he was near. Everything was hushed and still. No one dared to speak above a whisper. It was evening, and growing dark. As the men lay on the ground, keenly sensible to every sound, and anxiously waiting, they heard the firm tread of a man walking along the line. As he walked they heard also the jingle-jangle of a pile of canteens hung around his neck. He advanced with deliberate mien to within a few yards of the line and opened a terrific fight by quietly saying, "Can any you fellows tell a man whar he can git some water?" Instantly the thicket was illumined by the flash of a thousand muskets, the men leaped to their feet, the officers shouted, and the battle was begun. Neither side would yield, and there they fought till many died.

Soon, however, the reserve brigade began to make its way through the thicket. The first man to appear was the brigadier, thirty yards

ahead of his brigade, his sword between his
teeth, and parting the bushes with both hands
as he spurred his horse through the tangled
growth. Eager for the fight, his eyes glaring
and his countenance lit up with fury, his first
word was "Forward!" and forward went the
line.

THE BATTLE OPENS

On the march from Petersburg to Appomattox, after a sharp engagement, some men of
Cutshaw's artillery battalion, acting as infantry,
made a stand for a while on a piece of high
ground. They noticed, hanging around in a

lonely, distracted way, a tall, lean, shaggy fellow holding, or rather leaning on, a long staff, around which hung a faded battle-flag Thinking him out of his place and skulking, they suggested to him that it would be well for him to join his regiment. He replied that his regiment had all run away, and he was merely waiting a chance to be useful. Just then the enemy's advancing skirmishers poured a hot fire into the group, and the artillerymen began to discuss the propriety of leaving. The color-bearer, remembering their insinuations, saw an opportunity for retaliation. Standing, as he was, in the midst of a shower of musket balls, he seemed almost ready to fall asleep. But suddenly his face was illumined with a singularly pleased and childish smile. Quietly walking up close to the group, he said, "Any you boys want to *charge?*" The boys answered, "Yes." "Well," said the imperturbable, "I'm the man to carry this here old flag for you. Just follow me." So saying he led the squad full into the face of the advancing enemy, and never once seemed to think of stopping until he was urged to retire with the squad. He came back smiling from head to foot, and suffered no more insinuations.

At Gettysburg, when the artillery fire was at its height, a brawny fellow, who seemed happy

at the prospect for a hot time, broke out singing : —

"Backward, roll backward, O Time in thy flight:
Make me a child again, just for this *fight!*"

Another fellow near him replied, "Yes ; and
a *gal* child at that."

At Fredericksburg a good soldier, now a
farmer in Chesterfield County, Virginia, was
desperately wounded and lay on the field all
night. In the morning a surgeon approached
him and inquired the nature of his wound.
Finding a wound which is always considered
fatal, he advised the man to remain quietly
where he was and die. The man insisted on
being removed to a hospital, saying in the most
emphatic manner, that though every man ever
wounded as he was (his bowels were punctured
by the ball) had died, he was determined not
to die. The surgeon, struck by the man's courage and nerve, consented to remove him, ad-
vising him, however, not to cherish the hope of
recovery. After a hard struggle he did recover,
and is to-day a living example of the power of
a determined will.

At the Wilderness, when the fight was rag-
ing in the tangled woods and a man could
scarcely trust himself to move in any direction
for fear of going astray or running into the

hands of the enemy, a mere boy was wounded. Rushing out of the woods, his eyes staring and his face pale with fright, he shouted, " Where 's the rear. Mister! I say, Mister! where 's the rear?" Of course he was laughed at. The very grim fact that there was no " rear," in the sense of safety, made the question irresistibly ludicrous. The conduct of this boy was not exceptional. It was no uncommon thing to see the best men badly demoralized and eager to go to the rear because of a wound scarcely worthy of the name. On the other hand, it sometimes happened that men seriously wounded could not be convinced of their danger, and remained on the field.

The day General Stuart fell, mortally wounded, there was a severe fight in the woods not far from the old Brook Church, a few miles from Richmond; the enemy was making a determined stand, in order to gain time to repair a bridge which they were compelled to use, and the Confederate infantry skirmishers were pushing them hard. The fighting was stubborn and the casualties on the Confederate side very numerous. In the midst of the fight a voice was heard shouting, " Where 's my boy? I 'm looking for my boy!" Soon the owner of the voice appeared, tall, slim, aged, with silver gray hair, dressed in a full suit of broadcloth. A tall silk

hat and a clerical collar and cravat completed
his attire. His voice, familiar to the people of
Virginia, was deep and powerful. As he continued to shout, the men replied, " Go back, old
gentleman ; you 'll get hurt here. Go back ; go
back ! " " No, no ; " said he, " I can go anywhere my boy has to go, and the Lord is here.
I want to see my boy, and I will see him ! "
Then the order, " Forward ! " was given and the
men made once more for the enemy. The old
gentleman, his beaver in one hand, a big stick
in the other, his long hair flying, shouting,
" Come on, boys ! " disappeared in the depths of
the woods, well in front. He was a Methodist
minister, an old member of the Virginia Con-
ference, but his carriage that day was soldierly
and grand. One thought — that *his boy was
there* — made the old man feel that he might
brave the danger, too. No man who saw him
there will ever forget the parson who led the
charge at Brook Church.

At the battle of Spottsylvania Court House,
a gun in position somewhat in advance of the
line was so much exposed to the enemy's fire
that it was abandoned. Later in the day the
battery being ordered to move, the captain directed the sergeant to take his detachment and
bring in the gun. The sergeant and his gunner,
with a number of men, went out to bring in

the gun by hand.   Two men lifted the trail and the sergeant ordered, " All together ! "   The gun moved, but moved *in a circle.*   The fire was hot, and *all hands were on the same side* — the side farthest from the enemy !   After some persuasion the corporal and the sergeant managed to induce a man or two to get on the other side, with them, and they were moving along very comfortably when a shrapnel whacked the sergeant on his breast, breaking his ribs and tearing away the muscle of one arm.   He fell into the arms of the corporal.   Seeing that their only hope of escaping from this fire was work, the cannoniers bent to the wheels, and the gun rolled slowly to shelter.

It was at Spottsylvania Court House that the Federal infantry rushed over the works, and, engaging in a hand-to-hand fight, drove out the Confederate infantry.   On one part of the line the artillerymen stood to their posts, and when the Federal troops passing the works had massed themselves inside, fired to the right and left, up and down the lines, cutting roadways through the compact masses of men, and holding their positions until the Confederate infantry re-formed, drove out the enemy and re-occupied the line.   Several batteries were completely overrun, and the cannoniers sought and found safety *in front of the works,* whence the enemy had made their charge.

At another point on the lines, where there was no infantry support, the enemy charged repeatedly and made every effort to carry the works, but were handsomely repulsed by *artillery alone*. An examination of the ground in front of the works after the fight, disclosed the fact that all the dead and wounded were victims of artillery fire. The dead were literally torn to pieces, and the wounded dreadfully mangled. Scarcely a man was hurt on the Confederate side.

At Fort Harrison, a few miles below Richmond, in 1864, a ludicrous scene resulted from the firing of a salute with shotted guns. Federal artillery occupied the fort, and the lines immediately in front of it were held by the " Department Battalion," composed of the clerks in the various government offices in Richmond, who had been ordered out to meet an emergency. Just before sundown the detail for picket duty was formed, and about to march out to the picket line, the clerks presenting quite a soldierly appearance. Suddenly bang ! went a gun in the fort, and a shell came tearing over. Bang ! again, and bang ! bang ! and more shells exploding. Pow ! pow ! what consternation ! In an instant the beautiful line melted away as by magic. Every man took to shelter, and the place was desolate. The firing was rapid, regular, and apparently aimed to strike the Confederate lines, but ceased as suddenly as it had begun. General Custis Lee, whose tent was near by, observing the panic, stepped quietly up to the parapet of the works, folded his arms, and walked back and forth without uttering a word or looking to the right or to the left. His cool behavior, coupled with the silence of the guns, soon reassured the trembling clerks, and one by one they dropped into line again. General Butler had heard some news that pleased him, and ordered a salute with shotted guns. That was all.

Two boys who had volunteered for service with the militia in the same neighborhood, were detailed for picket duty. It was the custom to put three men on each post, — two militia boys and one veteran. The boys and an old soldier of Johnston's division were marched to their post, where they found, ready dug, a pit about five feet deep and three feet wide. It was quite dark, and the boys, realizing fully their exposed position, at once occupied the pit. The old soldier saw he had an opportunity to have a good time, knowing that those boys would keep wide awake. Giving them a short lecture about the importance of great watchfulness, he warned them to be ready to leave there very rapidly at any moment, and, above all, to keep very quiet.

His words were wasted, as the boys would not
have closed their eyes or uttered a word for the
world. These little details arranged, the cun-
ning old soldier prepared to make himself comfortable. First he gathered a few small twigs
and made a *very small* fire. On the fire he put
a battered old tin cup. Into this he poured some
coffee from his canteen. From some mysterious
place in his clothes he drew forth sugar and
dropped it into the cup. Next, from an old
worn haversack, he took a "chunk" of raw
bacon and a "pone" of corn bread. Then,
drawing a large pocket knife, in a dexterous
manner he sliced and ate his bread and meat,
occasionally sipping his coffee. His evening
meal leisurely completed, he filled his pipe,
smoked, and stirred up the imaginations of the
boys by telling how dangerous a duty they were
performing; told them how easy it would be
for the Yankees to creep up and shoot them or
capture and carry them off. Having finished his
smoke, he knocked out the ashes and dropped
the pipe in his pocket. Then he actually un-
rolled his blanket and oil-cloth. It made the
perspiration start on the brows of the boys to
see the man's folly. Then taking off his shoes,
he laid down on one edge, took hold of the
blanket and oil-cloth, rolled himself over to the
other side, and with a kind "good night" to

8

the boys, began to snore.　The poor boys stood like statues in the pit till broad day.　In the morning the old soldier thanked them for not disturbing him, and quietly proceeded to prepare his breakfast.

After the fight at Fisher's Hill, in 1864, Early's army, in full retreat and greatly demoralized, was strung out along the valley pike. The Federal cavalry was darting around picking up prisoners, shooting drivers, and making themselves generally disagreeable.　It happened that an artilleryman, who was separated from his gun, was making pretty good time on foot, getting to the rear, and had the *appearance* of a demoralized infantryman who had thrown away his musket.　So one of these lively cavalrymen trotted up, and, waving his sabre, told the artilleryman to "surrender!"　But he did n't stop.　He merely glanced over his shoulder, and kept on.　Then the cavalryman became indignant and shouted, "Halt, d——n you; halt!"　And still he would not.　"Halt," said the cavalryman, "halt, you d——n s— of a ——; halt!"　Then the artilleryman halted, and remarking that he did n't allow any man to speak to *him* that way, seized a huge stick, turned on the cavalryman, knocked him out of his saddle, and proceeded on his journey to the rear.

This artilleryman fought with a musket at Sailor's Creek. He found himself surrounded by the enemy, who demanded surrender. He refused; said they must take him; and laid about him with the butt of his musket till he had damaged some of the party considerably. He was, however, overpowered and made a prisoner.

Experienced men, in battle, always availed themselves of any shelter within reach. A tree, a fence, a mound of earth, a ditch, anything. Sometimes their efforts to find shelter were very amusing and even silly. Men lying on the ground have been seen to put an old canteen before their heads as a shelter from musket balls; and during a heavy fire of artillery, seemed to feel safer *under a tent*. Only recruits and fools neglected the smallest shelter.

The more experienced troops knew better when to give up than green ones, and never fought well after they were satisfied that they could not accomplish their purpose. Consequently it often happened that the best troops failed where the raw ones did well. The old Confederate soldier *would* decide some questions for himself. To the last he maintained the right of private judgment, and especially on the field of battle.

CHAPTER VIII.

SUNDAY, April 2, 1865, found Cutshaw's battalion of artillery occupying the earthworks at Fort Clifton on the Appomattox, about two miles below Petersburg, Virginia. The command was composed of the Second Company Richmond Howitzers, Captain Lorraine F. Jones, Garber's battery, Fry's battery, and remnants of five other batteries (saved from the battle of Spottsylvania Court House, May 12, 1864), and had present for duty nearly five hundred men, with a total muster-roll, including the men in prison, of one thousand and eighty.

The place — the old " Clifton House " — was well fortified, and had the additional protection of the river along the entire front of perhaps a mile. The works extended from the Appomattox on the right to Swift Creek on the left. There were some guns of heavy calibre mounted and ready for action, and in addition to these some field-pieces disposed along the line at suitable points. The enemy had formidable works opposite, but had not used their guns to disturb the quiet routine of the camp. The river bank was picketed by details from the artillery, armed as infantry, but without the usual equipments. The guard duty was so heavy that half the men were always on guard.

The huts, built by the troops who had formerly occupied the place, were located, with a view to protection from the enemy's fire, under the hills on the sides of the ravines or gullies which divided them, and were underground to the eaves of the roof. Consequently, the soil being sandy, there was a constant filtering of sand through the cracks, and in spite of the greatest care, the grit found its way into the flour and meal, stuck to the greasy frying-pan, and even filled the hair of the men as they slept in their bunks.

At this time rations were reduced to the minimum of quantity and quality, being generally worm-eaten peas, sour or rancid mess-pork, and unbolted corn meal, relieved occasionally with a small supply of luscious canned beef, imported from England, good flour (half rations), a little coffee and sugar, and, once, apple brandy for all hands. Ragged, barefooted, and even bareheaded men were so common that they did not excite notice or comment, and did not expect or seem to feel the want of sympathy. And yet there was scarcely a complaint or murmur of dissatisfaction, and not the slightest indication of fear or doubt. The spirit of the men was as good as ever, and the possibility of immediate disaster had not cast its shadow there.

Several incidents occurred during the stay of the battalion at Fort Clifton which will serve to illustrate every-day life on the lines. It occurred to a man picketing the river bank that it would be amusing to take careful aim at the man on the other side doing the same duty for the enemy, fire, laugh to see the fellow jump and dodge, and then try again. He fired, laughed, dropped his musket to reload, and while smiling with satisfaction, heard the "thud" of a bullet and felt an agonizing pain in his arm. His musket fell to the ground, and he walked back to camp with his arm swinging heavily at his side. The surgeon soon relieved him of it altogether. The poor fellow learned a lesson. The "Yank" had beat him at his own game.

The guard-house was a two-story framed building, about twelve feet square, having two rooms, one above the other. The detail for guard duty was required to stay in the guard-house; those who wished to sleep going upstairs, while others just relieved or about to go on duty clustered around the fire in the lower room. One night, when the upper floor was

covered with sleeping men, an improvised infantryman who had been relieved from duty
walked in, and, preparatory to taking his stand
at the fire, threw his musket carelessly in the
corner. A loud report and angry exclamations
immediately followed. The sergeant of the
guard, noticing the direction of the ball, hurried up-stairs, and to the disgust of the sleepy
fellows, ordered all hands to " turn out." Grum-
bling, growling, stretching, and rubbing their
eyes, the men got up. Some one inquired,
" Where 's Pryor ? " His chum, who had been
sleeping by his side, replied, " there he is, asleep ;
shake him." His blanket was drawn aside, and
with a shake he was commanded to " get up ! "
But there was no motion, no reply. The ball
had passed through his heart, and he had passed
without a groan or a sigh from deep sleep to
death. The man who was killed and the man
who was sleeping by his side under the same
blanket, were members of the Second Company
Richmond Howitzers. The careless man who
made the trouble was also an artilleryman, from
one of the other batteries.

Shortly after this accident, after a quiet day,
the men retired to their huts, and the whole
camp was still as a country church-yard. The
pickets on the river's edge could hear those on
the opposite side asking the corporal of the

guard the hour, and complaining that they had
not been promptly relieved. Suddenly a terrific bombardment commenced, and the earth
fairly trembled. The men, suddenly awakened,
heard the roar of the guns, the rush of the
shots, and the explosion of the shells. To a
man only half awake, the shells seemed to pass
very near and in every direction. In a moment
all were rushing out of their houses, and soon
the hill-sides and bluffs were covered with an
excited crowd, gazing awe-struck on the sight.
The firing was away to the right, and there was
not the slightest danger. Having realized this
fact, the interest was intense. The shells from
the opposite lines met and passed in mid-air —
their burning fuses forming an arch of fire,
which paled occasionally as a shell burst, illu-
minating the heavens with its blaze. The uproar, even at such a distance, was terrible. The
officers, fearing that fire would be opened along
the whole line, ordered the cannoniers to their
posts ; men were sent down into the magazine
with lanterns to arrange the ammunition for
the heavy guns ; the lids of the limbers of the
field-pieces were thrown up ; the cannoniers
were counted off at their posts ; the brush which
had been piled before the embrasures was torn
away ; and, with implements in hand, all stood
at "attention !" till the last shot was fired.

The heavens were dark again, and silence reigned. Soon all hands were as sound asleep as though nothing had occurred.

The next morning an artilleryman came walking leisurely towards the camp, and being recognized as belonging to a battery which was in position on that part of the line where the firing of the last night occurred, was plied with questions as to the loss on our side, who was hurt, etc., etc. Smiling at the anxious faces and eager questions, he replied: "When? Last night? Nobody!" It was astounding, but nevertheless true.

On another occasion some scattering shots were heard up the river, and after a while a body came floating down the stream. It was hauled on shore and buried in the sand a little above high-water mark. It was a poor Confederate who had attempted to desert to the enemy, but was shot while swimming for the opposite bank of the river. His grave was the centre of the beat of one of the picket posts on the river bank, and there were few men so indifferent to the presence of the dead as not to prefer some other post.

And so, while there had been no fighting, there were always incidents to remind the soldier that danger lurked around, and that he could not long avoid his share. The camp was

not as joyous as it had been, and all felt that
the time was near which would try the courage
of the stoutest. The struggles of the troops on
the right with overwhelming numbers and re-
ports of adversities, caused a general expectation that the troops lying so idly at the Clifton
House would be ordered to the point of danger.
They had not long to wait.

Sunday came and went as many a Sunday
had. There was nothing unusual apparent, unless, perhaps, the dull and listless attitudes of
the men, and the monotonous call of those on
guard were more oppressive than usual. The
sun went down, the hills and valleys and the
river were veiled in darkness. Here and there
twinkling lights were visible. On the other side
of the river could be heard a low rumbling
which experienced men said was the movement
of artillery and ammunition trains bound to the
enemy's left to press the already broken right
of the Confederate line.

Some had actually gone to sleep for the night.
Others were huddled around the fires in the
little huts, and a few sat out on the hill-side dis-
cussing the probabilities of the near future.
A most peaceful scene ; a most peaceful spot.
Hymns were sung and prayers were made,
though no preacher was there. Memory re-
verted fondly to the past, to home and friends.

The spirit of the soldier soared away to other scenes, and left *him* to sit blankly down, gaze at the stars, and feel unspeakable longings for undefined joys, and weep, for very tenderness of heart, at his own sad loneliness.

At ten P. M. some man mounted on horseback rode up to one of the huts, and said the battalion had orders to move. It was so dark that his face was scarcely visible. In a few minutes orders were received to destroy what could be destroyed without noise or fire. This was promptly done. Then the companies were formed, the roll was called, and the battalion marched slowly and solemnly away. No one doubted that the command would march at once to the assistance of the troops at or near Five Forks. It was thought that before morning every man would have his musket and his supply of ammunition, and the crack of day would see the battalion rushing into battle in regular infantry style, whooping and yelling like demons. But they got no arms that night. The march was steady till broad day of Monday the 3d of April. Of course the men felt mortified at having to leave the guns, but there was no help for it, as the battery horses which had been sent away to winter had not returned. It was evident that the battalion had bid farewell to artillery, and commenced a new career as infantry.

As the night wore on the men learned that the command was not going to any point on the lines. That being determined, no one could guess its destination. Later in the night, probably as day approached, the sky in the direction of Richmond was lit with the red glare of distant conflagration, and at short intervals there were deep, growling explosions of magazines. The roads were filled with other troops, all hurrying in the same direction. There was no sign of panic or fear, but the very wheels seemed turning with unusual energy. The men wore the look of determination, haste, and eagerness. One could feel the energy which surrounded him and animated the men and things which moved so steadily on, on, on! There was no laughing, singing, or talking. Nothing but the steady tread of the column and the surly rumbling of the trains.

As morning dawned the battalion struck the main road leading from Richmond. Refugees told the story of the evacuation, and informed the boys from the city that it was in the hands of the enemy and burning, and the chances were that not one house would be left standing. Here it became clearly understood that the whole army was in full retreat. From this point the men began to say, as they marched, that it was easier to march away than it would

be to get back, but that they expected **and**
hoped to *fight* their way back if they had **to**
contest every inch. Some even regretted the
celerity of the march, for, they said, "the further we march the more difficult it will be to
win our way back." Little did they know of
the immense pressure at the rear, and the earnest push of the enemy on the flank as he
strove to reach and overlap the advance of his
hitherto defiant, but now retreating, foe.

A detail had been left at Fort Clifton with
orders to spike the guns, blow up the magazine,
destroy everything which could be of value to
the enemy, and rejoin the command. The order was obeyed, and every man of the detail
resumed his place in the ranks.

From this point to Appomattox the march
was almost continuous, day and night, and it is
with the greatest difficulty that a private in the
ranks can recall with accuracy the dates and
places on the march. Night was day — day
was night. There was no stated time to sleep,
eat, or rest, and the events of morning became
strangely intermingled with the events of evening. Breakfast, dinner, and supper were
merged into "something to eat," whenever and
wherever it could be had. The incidents of the
march, however, lose none of their significance
on this account, and so far as possible they will

be given in the order in which they occurred, and the day and hour fixed as accurately as they can be by those who witnessed and participated in its dangers and hardships.

Monday, the 3d, the column was pushed along without ceremony, at a rapid pace, until night, when a halt was ordered and the battalion laid down in a piece of pine woods to rest. There was some " desultory " eating in this camp, but so little of it that there was no lasting effect. At early dawn of Tuesday, the 4th, the men struggled to their feet, and with empty stomachs and brave hearts resumed their places in the ranks, and struggled on with the column as it marched steadily in the direction of Moore's Church, in Amelia County, where it arrived in the night. The men laid down under the shelter of a fine grove, and friend divided with friend the little supplies of raw bacon and bread picked up on the day's march. They were scarcely stretched on the ground ready for a good nap, when the orderly of the Howitzers commenced bawling, " Detail for guard ! detail for guard ! Fall in here; fall in ! " then followed the names of the detail. Four men answered to their names, but declared they could not keep awake if placed on guard. Their remonstrance was in vain. They were marched off to picket a road leading to camp, and when they were relieved, said they had slept soundly on their posts. No one blamed them.

While it was yet night all hands were roused from profound sleep; the battalion was formed, and away they went, stumbling, bumping against each other, and *sleeping as they walked.* Whenever the column halted for a moment, as it did frequently during the night, the men dropped heavily to the ground and were instantly asleep. Then the officers would commence: " Forward! column forward! " Those first on their feet went stumbling on over their prostrate comrades, who would in turn be awakened, and again the column was in motion, and nothing heard but the monotonous tread of the weary feet, the ringing and rattling of the trappings of the horses, and the never-ending cry of " Close up, men ; close up! "

Through the long, weary night there was no rest. The alternate halting and hurrying was terribly trying, and taxed the endurance of the most determined men to the very utmost; and yet on the morning of Wednesday, the 5th, when the battalion reached the neighborhood of Scott's Shops, every man was in place and ready for duty. From this point, after some ineffectual efforts to get a breakfast, the column pushed on in the direction of Amelia Court House, at which point Colonel Cutshaw was ordered to report to General James A. Walker, and the battalion was thereafter a part of Walker's division. The 5th was spent at or near the court house — how, it is difficult to remember; but the day was marked by several incidents worthy of record.

About two hundred and twenty-five muskets (not enough to arm all the men), cartridges, and caps were issued to the battalion — simply the muskets and ammunition. Not a cartridge-box, cap-box, belt, or any other convenience ornamented the persons of these new-born infantrymen. They stored their ammunition in their pockets along with their corn, salt, pipes, and tobacco.

When application was made for rations, it was found that the last morsel belonging to the division had been issued to the command, and the battalion was again thrown on its own resources, to wit: corn on the cob intended for the horses. Two ears were issued to each man. It was parched in the coals, mixed with salt, stored in the pockets, and eaten on the road. Chewing the corn was hard work. It made the jaws ache and the gums and teeth so sore as to cause almost unendurable pain.

After the muskets were issued a line of battle was formed with Cutshaw on the right. For what purpose the line was formed the men could not tell. A short distance from the right of the line there was a grove which concealed an ammunition train which had been sent from Richmond to meet the army. The ammunition had been piled up ready for destruction. An occasional musket ball passed over near enough and often enough to produce a realizing sense of the proximity of the enemy and solemnize the occasion. Towards evening the muskets were stacked, artillery style of course, the men were lying around, chatting and eating raw bacon, and there was general quiet, when suddenly the earth shook with a tremendous explosion and an immense column of smoke rushed up into the air to a great height. For a moment there was the greatest consternation. Whole regiments broke and fled in wild confusion. Cutshaw's men stood up, seized their muskets, and stood at attention till it was known that the ammunition had been purposely fired and no enemy was threatening the line. Then what laughter and hilarity prevailed, for a while, among these famishing men !

Order having been restored, the march was resumed, and moving by way of Amelia Springs, the column arrived near Deatonsville, about ten o'clock, on the morning of Thursday the 6th. The march, though not a long one, was exceedingly tiresome, as, the main roads being crowded, the column moved by plantation roads, which were in wretched condition and crowded with troops and trains. That the night was spent in the most trying manner may best be learned from the fact that when morning dawned the column was only six or seven miles from the starting point of the evening before.

This delay was fatal. The whole army — trains and all — left Amelia Court House in advance of Walker's division, which was left to cover the retreat, Cutshaw's battalion being the last to leave the court house, thus bringing up the rear of the army, and being in constant view of the enemy's hovering cavalry. The movement of the division was regulated to suit the movements of the wagon trains, which should have been destroyed on the spot, and the column allowed to make its best time, as, owing to the delay they occasioned, the army lost the time it had gained on the enemy in the start, and was overtaken the next day.

At Deatonsville another effort to cook was made, but before the simplest articles of food could be prepared, the order to march was given, and the battalion took the road once more.

A short while after passing Deatonsville the column was formed in line of battle, — Cutshaw's battalion near the road and in an old

field with woods in front and rear. The officers, anticipating an immediate attack, ordered
the men to do what they could for their protection. They immediately scattered along the
fence on the roadside, and taking down the rails
stalked back to their position in line, laid the
rails on the ground and returned for another
load. This they continued to do until the
whole of the fence was removed. Behind this
slim defense they silently awaited the advance
of the enemy.

Soon it was decided that this was not the
place to make a stand. The first detachment of
the Second Company of Richmond Howitzers,
and twenty men each from Garber and Fry,
under the command of Lieutenant Henry Jones,
were left behind the fence-rail work, with orders
to resist and retard the advance of the enemy
while the column continued its march.

This little band was composed of true spirits,
— the best material in the battalion. Right well
did they do their duty. Left alone to face the
advance of the immense host eagerly pursuing
the worn remnant of the invincible army, they
waited until the enemy's skirmishers appeared
in the field, when, with perfect deliberation,
they commenced their fire. Though greatly
outnumbered, and flanked right and left, they
stubbornly held on till the line of battle follow-

ing the skirmishers broke from the woods, and advancing rapidly poured into them a murderous volley. And yet, so unused were they to running, they moved not till the infantry skirmishers had retired, and the word of command was heard. Then stubbornly contesting the ground, they fought their way back through the woods. The gallant Lieutenant Jones fell mortally wounded, having held control of his little band to the moment he fell. His friend Kemp refused to leave him, and they were captured together, but were immediately separated by the enemy. Pearson was pierced through by a musket ball as he was hurrying through the woods, and fell heavily to the ground. Binford was severely wounded, but managed to escape. Hamilton was killed outright.

The battalion had left this point but a short time, marching in column of fours with the division, and had reached the brow of a gently sloping hill, perfectly open for perhaps a mile, with a broad valley on the left, and beyond it a range of hills partly wooded. In an open space on this range the enemy placed a battery in position, and, in anticipation of doing great slaughter from a safe distance, opened a rapid fire on the exposed and helpless column. The shells came hurtling over the valley, exploding in front, rear, and overhead, and tearing up the ground in every direction. Ah! how it grieved those artillerymen to stand, musket in hand, and receive that shower of insolence. How they longed for the old friends they had left at Fort Clifton. They knew how those rascals on the other side of the valley were enjoying the sport. They could hear, in imagination, the shouts of the cannoniers as they saw their shells bursting so prettily, and rammed home another shot.

There was some impediment ahead, and there the column stood, a fair mark for these rascals. There was no help near, and all that could be done was to stand firm and wait orders; but help was coming.

A cloud of dust was approaching from the rear of the column. All eyes were strained to see what it might mean. Presently the artillerymen recognized a well-known sound. A battery was coming in full gallop, the drivers lashing their horses and yelling like madmen. The guns bounded along as though they would outrun the horses, and with rush, roar, and rattle they approached the front of the battalion. Some fellow in the Second Company Howitzers sung out, " Old Henry Carter! Hurrah! for the Third Company! Give it to 'em, boys!" It was, indeed, the Third Company of Howitzers, long separated from the Second, with their gallant captain at their head!

Not a moment was lost. The guns were in battery, and the smoke of the first shot was curling about the heads of the men in the column in marvelously quick time. Friends and comrades in the column called to the men at the guns, and they, as they stepped in and out, responded with cheerful, ringing voices, " Hello, Bill!" " How are you, Joe?" Bang! " Pretty " — Bang! — " well, I thank you." Bang! " Oh! we 're giving it to 'em now." Bang!

As the battalion moved on, the gallant boys of the Third Company finished their work. The disappointed enemy limbered up, slipped into the woods and departed. Cheered by this fortunate meeting with old comrades, with the pleasant odor of the smoke lingering around them, these hitherto bereft and mournful artillerymen pushed on, laughing at the discomfiture of the enemy, and feeling that though deprived of their guns by the misfortunes of war, there was still left at least one battery worthy to represent the artillery of the army.

As the column marched slowly along, some sharp-eyed man discovered three of the enemy's skirmishers in a field away on the left. More for amusement than anything else, it was proposed to fire at them. A group of men gathered on the roadside, a volley was fired, and, to the amazement of the marksmen, for the distance was great, one of the skirmishers fell. One of his comrades started on a run to his assistance, and he, too, was stopped. The third man then scampered away as fast as his legs could carry him. The battalion applauded the good shots and marched on.

At Sailor's Creek the detachment which had been left at Deatonsville, behind the fence rails, to watch and retard the approach of the enemy, having slowly retired before their advance, rejoined the command. Indeed, their resistance and retreat was the beginning of and ended in the battle of Sailor's Creek.

The line of battle was formed on Locket's Hill, which sloped gently down from the line to the creek, about one hundred and fifty or two hundred yards in rear of and running nearly parallel with the line of battle. A road divided the battalion near the centre. The Howitzers were on the left of this road and in the woods; Garber's men were on the right of the Howitzers, on the opposite side of the road, in a field; Fry's men on the extreme left. To cross the road dividing the line was a hazardous experiment, as the enemy, thinking it an important avenue, swept it with musketry.

It was amusing to see the men hauling out of their pockets a mixture of corn, salt, caps, and cartridges, and, selecting the material needed, loading. They were getting ready to stand. They did not expect to run, and did not until ordered to do so.

The enemy's skirmishers advanced confidently and in rather free and easy style, but suddenly met a volley which drove them to cover. Again they advanced, in better order, and again the improvised infantry forced them back. Then came their line of battle with overwhelming numbers ; but the battalion stubbornly resisted their advance. The men, not accustomed to the orderly manner of infantry, dodged about from tree to tree, and with the deliberation of huntsmen picked off here and there a man. When a shot "told," the marksman hurrahed, all to himself. There was an evident desire to press forward and drive the advancing foe. Several of the men were so enthusiastic that they had pushed ahead of the line, and several yards in advance they could be seen loading and firing as deliberately as though practicing at a mark.

Colonel Cutshaw received a wound which so shattered his leg that he had to be lifted from his horse into an ambulance. He was near being captured, but by hurrying away the ambulance at a gallop, he escaped to a house a short distance in the rear, where he fell into the hands of the enemy. The same night he suffered amputation of a leg. Captain Garber was struck, and called for the ambulance corps, but on examination found the ball in his pocket. It had lodged against the rowel of a spur which he found the day before and dropped in his pocket.

At last the enemy appeared in strong force on both flanks, while he pushed hard in front. It was useless to attempt a further stand. The voice of Captain Jones, of the Howitzers, rang out loud and clear, " Boys, take care of yourselves ! " Saying this, he planted himself against a pine, and, as his men rushed by him, emptied every chamber of his revolver at the enemy, and then reluctantly made his way, in company with several privates, down the hill to the creek.

At the foot of the hill a group of perhaps a dozen men gathered around Lieutenant McRae. He was indignant. He proposed another stand, and his comrades agreed. They stood in the road, facing the gentle slope of the hill from which they had been ordered to retire. The enemy's skirmishers were already on the brow of the hill, dodging about among the trees and shouting to those behind to hurry up. Their favorite expressions were, "Come along, boys; here are the damned rebel wagons ! " "Damn 'em, shoot 'em down ! "

In a few moments their line of battle, in beautiful order, stepped out of the woods with colors flying, and for a moment halted. In front of the centre of that portion of the line which was visible — probably a full regimental front — marched the colors, and color-guard. McRae

LAST SHOT. SAILOR'S CREEK.

saw his opportunity. He ordered his squad to rise and fire on the colors. His order was promptly obeyed. The color-bearer pitched forward and fell, with his colors, heavily to the ground The guard of two men on either side shared the same fate, or else feigned it. Immediately the line of battle broke into disorder, and came swarming down the hill, firing, yelling, and cursing as they came. An officer, mounted, rode his horse close to the fence on the roadside, and with the most superb insolence mocked McRae and his squad, already, as he thought, hopelessly intermingled with the enemy. McRae, in his rage, swore back at him, and in the hearing of the man, called on a man near him to shoot "that —— ——," calling him a fearfully hard name. But the private's gun was not in working order, and the fellow escaped for the time. Before he reached the woods, whither he was going to hurry up the "boys," a Howitzer let fly at him, and at the shock of the bullet's stroke he threw his arms up in the air, and his horse bore him into the woods a corpse.

A little to the left, where the road crossed the creek, the crack of pistols and the " bang " of muskets was continuous. The enemy had surrounded the wagons and were mercilessly shooting down the unarmed and helpless drivers, some of whom, however, managed to cut the traces, mount, and ride away.

In order to escape from the right of the line, it was necessary to follow the road, which was along the foot of the hill, some distance to the left. The enemy seeing this were pushing their men rapidly at a right oblique to gain the road and cut off retreat. Consequently those who attempted escape in that direction had to run the gauntlet of a constant fusilade from a mass of troops near enough to select individuals, curse them, and command them to throw down their arms or be shot.

Most of McRae's squad, in spite of the difficulties surrounding them, gained the creek, plunged in, and began a race for life up the long, open hill-side of plowed ground, fired upon at every step by the swarm of men behind, and before they reached the top, by a battery in close proximity, which poured down a shower of canister.

The race to the top of the long hill was exceedingly trying to men already exhausted by continual marching, hunger, thirst, and loss of sleep. They ran, panting for breath, like chased animals, fairly staggering as they went.

On the top of this long hill there was a skirmish line of cavalry posted, with orders to stop all men with arms in their hands, and form a new line; but the view down the hill to the creek and beyond revealed such a host of the enemy, and the men retiring before them were so few, that the order was disregarded and the fleeing band allowed to pass through.

The men's faces were black with powder. They had bitten cartridges until there was a deep black circle around their mouths. The burnt powder from the ramrods had blackened their hands, and in their efforts to remove the perspiration from their faces they had completed the coloring from the roots of the hair to the chin. Here was no place for rest, however, as the enemy's battery behind the creek on the opposite hills, having gotten the range, was pouring in a lively fire. Soon after passing the brow of the hill darkness came on. Groups of men from the battalion halted on the roadside, near a framed building of some sort, and commenced shouting, " Fall in, Howitzers ! " " This way, Garber's men ! " " Fry's battery ! " " Fall in ! " " Cutshaw's battalion, fall in here ! " thus of their own accord trying to recover the organization from its disorder. Quite a number of the battalion got together, and in spite of hunger, thirst, defeat, and dreadful weariness, pushed on to the High Bridge. So anxious were the men to escape capture and the insinuation of desertion, that when threatened with shooting by the rear guard if they did not move on they scarcely turned to see who spoke : but the simple announcement, " The Yankees are coming ! " gave them a little new strength, and again they struggled painfully along, dropping in the road sound asleep, however, at the slightest halt of the column.

At the bridge there was quite a halt, and in the darkness the men commenced calling to each other by name — the rascally infantry around, still ready for fun, answering for every name. Brother called brother, comrade called comrade, friend called friend ; and there were many happy reunions there that night. Some alas ! of the best and bravest did not answer the cry of anxious friends.

Before the dawn of day the column was again in motion. What strange sensations the men had as they marched slowly across the High Bridge. They knew its great height, but the night was so dark that they could not see the abyss on either side. Arrived on the other side, the worn-out soldiers fell to the ground and slept, more dead than alive. Some had slept as they marched across the bridge, and declared that they had no distinct recollection of when they left it, or how long they were upon it.

Early on the morning of the 7th the march

was resumed and continued through Farmville, across the bridge and to Cumberland Heights, overlooking the town. Here, on the bare hillside, a line of battle was formed, for what purpose the men did not know — the Howitzers occupying a central place in the line, and standing with their feet in the midst of a number of the graves of soldiers who had perished in the hospitals in the town.

While standing thus in line a detail was sent into the town to hunt up some rations. They found a tierce of bacon surrounded by a ravenous crowd, fighting and quarreling. The man on duty guarding the bacon was quickly overpowered, and the bacon distributed to the crowd. The detail secured a piece and marched back triumphantly to their waiting comrades.

After considerable delay the line broke into column and marched away in the direction of Curdsville. It was on this march that Cutshaw's battalion showed itself proof against the demoralization which was appearing, and received, almost from the lips of the Commander-in-Chief, a compliment of which any regiment in the army might be proud.

All along the line of march the enemy's cavalry followed close on the flanks of the column, and whenever an opportunity offered swooped down upon the trains. Whenever this occurred

the battalion, with the division, was faced towards the advancing cavalry, and marched in
line to meet them, generally repulsing them
with ease. In one of these attacks the cavalry
approached so near the column that a dash was
made at them, and the infantry returned to the
road with General Gregg, of the enemy's cavalry, a prisoner. He was splendidly equipped
and greatly admired by the ragged crowd
around him. He was, or pretended to be,
greatly surprised at his capture. When the
column had reached a point two or three miles
beyond Farmville, it was found that the enemy
was driving in the force which was protecting
the marching column and trains. The troops
hurrying back were panic-stricken; all efforts
to rally them were vain, and the enemy was
almost upon the column. General Gordon ordered General Walker to form his division and
drive the enemy back from the road. The
division advanced gallantly, and conspicuous in
the charge was Cutshaw's battalion. When
the line was formed, the battalion occupied rising ground on the right. The line was visible
for a considerable distance. In rear of the battalion there was a group of unarmed men under
command of Sergeant Ellett, of the Howitzers.
In the distribution of muskets at Amelia Court
House the supply fell short of the demand, and

this squad had made the trip so far unarmed. Some, too, had been compelled to ground their arms at Sailor's Creek. A few yards to the left and rear of the battalion, in the road, was General Lee, surrounded by a number of officers, gazing eagerly about him. An occasional musket ball whistled over, but there was no enemy in sight. In the midst of this quiet a general officer, at the left and rear of the battalion, fell from his horse, severely wounded. A messenger was sent from the group in the road to ask the extent of his injury. After a short while the enemy appeared, and the stampeded troops came rushing by. Cutshaw's battalion stood firmly and quietly, as if on parade, awaiting orders. General officers galloped about, begging the fleeing men to halt, but in vain. Several of the fugitives, as they passed the battalion, were collared by the disarmed squad, relieved of their muskets and ammunition, and with a kick allowed to proceed to the rear. There was now between the group in the road and the enemy only the battalion of improvised infantry. There they stood, on the crest of the hill, in sharp relief. Not a man moved from his place. Did they know the Great Commander was watching them? Some one said, " Forward ! " The cry passed from lip to lip, and, with cheers, the battalion moved

10

rapidly to meet the enemy, while the field was full of the stampeded troops making to the rear. A courier came out with orders to stop the advance, but they heeded him not. Again he came, but on they went. Following the line was the unarmed squad, unable to do more than swell the volume of the wild shouts of their comrades. Following them, also, was the commissary department, consisting of two men, with a piece of bacon swung on a pole between them, yelling and hurrahing. As the line advanced, the blue-jackets sprang up and ran through the broom-straw like hares, followed by a shower of balls. Finally an officer — some say General Gordon, and others an aide of Longstreet's — rode out to the front of the battalion, ordered a halt, and in the name of General Lee thanked the men for their gallant conduct and complimented them in handsome style. His words were greeted with loud cheers, and the battalion marched back to the road carrying several prisoners and having retaken two pieces of artillery which had been abandoned to the enemy. After the enemy was driven back out of reach of our trains and column of march, and the troops were in line of battle, General Lee in person rode up in rear of the division, and addressing himself directly to the men in ranks (a thing very unusual with him) used language to this effect: " That is right, men; that is all I want you to do. Just keep *those people* back awhile. I do not wish you to expose yourselves to unnecessary danger." Mahone's division then coming up took the place of Walker's, and the march was resumed. The battalion passed on, the men cutting slices from their piece of bacon and eagerly devouring them. As night came on the signs of disaster increased.

At several places whole trains were standing in the road abandoned; artillery, chopped down and burning, blocked the way, and wagonloads of ammunition were dumped out in the road and trampled under foot. There were abundant signs of disaster. So many muskets were dropped on the road that Cutshaw's unarmed squad *armed itself* with abandoned muskets, ammunition, and equipments.

There was a halt during the night in a piece of stunted woods. The land was low and sobby. In the road passing through the woods were several batteries, chopped down and deserted. There was a little flour on hand, which had been picked up on the road. An oil-cloth was spread, the flour placed on it, water was found, and the dough mixed. Then some clean partition boards were knocked out of a limber chest, the dough was spread on them and held near he fire till partially cooked. Then with what delight it was devoured !

At daybreak, Saturday, the march was resumed, and continued almost without interruption during the whole day; the men, those whose gums and teeth were not already too sore, crunching parched corn and raw bacon as they trudged along. Saturday night the battalion rested near Appomattox Court House, in a pine woods. Sunday morning, April 9th, after a short march, the column entered the village of Appomattox Court House by what seemed to be the main road. Several dead men, dressed in the uniform of United States regular artillery, were lying on the roadside, their faces turned up to the blaze of the sun. One had a ghastly wound in the breast, which must have been made by grape or canister.

On through the village without halting marched the column. "Whitworth" shots went hurtling through the air every few minutes, indicating very clearly that the enemy was ahead of the column and awaiting its arrival. On the outskirts of the village the line of battle was formed. Indeed, there seemed to be *two* lines, one slightly in advance of the other. Wagons passed along the line and dropped boxes of cartridges. The men were ordered to knock them open and supply themselves with forty rounds each. They filled their breeches' pockets to the brim. The general officers galloped up and down the line, apparently hurrying everything as much as possible. The shots from a battery in advance were continually passing over the line, going in the direction of the village, but without harm to any one. The more experienced men predicted a severe struggle. It was supposed that this was to be an attack with the whole army in mass, for the purpose of breaking through the enemy's line and making one more effort to move on.

Finally the order " Forward ! " ran along the line, and as it advanced the chiefs of detachments, gunners, and commissioned officers marched in rear, keeping up a continual cry of " Close up, men ; close up ! " " Go ahead, now ; don't lag ! " " Keep up ! " Thus marching, the line entered a body of woods, proceeded some distance, changed direction to the left, and, emerging from the woods, halted in a large open field, beyond which was another body of woods which concealed further view in front.

After some delay, a detail for skirmish duty was ordered. Captain Jones detailed four men, Fry and Garber the same number. Lieutenant McRae was placed in command. The infantry detailed skirmishers for their front. All arrangements completed, the men deployed and entered the woods. They had advanced but a short distance, when they encountered a strong line of picket posts. Firing and cheering they rushed on the surprised men, who scampered away, leaving all their little conveniences behind them, and retreating for about a mile. From this point large bodies of the enemy were visible, crowding the hill-tops like a blue or black cloud. It was not many minutes before a strong line of dismounted cavalry, followed by mounted men, deployed from this mass to cover the retreat of their fleeing brethren, and restore the picket line. They came down the hills and across the fields, firing as they came. On looking around to see what were the chances for making a stand, Lieutenant McRae found that the infantry skirmishers had been withdrawn. The officer who had commanded them could be seen galloping away in the distance. The little squad, knowing they were alone, kept up a brisk fire on the advancing enemy, till he was close up in front, and well to the rear of both flanks. On the left, not more than two hundred yards, a column of cavalry, marching by twos, had crossed the line and were still marching, as unconcernedly as possible, to the rear of McRae. Seeing this, McRae ordered his squad to retire, saying at the same time, " But don't let them see you running, boys!"

So they retired, slowly, stubbornly, and returning shot for shot with the enemy, who came on at a trot, cheering valiantly, as they pursued four men and a lieutenant. The men dragged the butts of their old muskets behind them, loading as they walked. All loaded, they turned, halted, fired, received a shower of balls in return, and then again moved doggedly to the rear. A little lieutenant of infantry, who had been on the skirmish line, joined the squad. He was armed with a revolver, and had his sword by his side. Stopping behind the corner of a corn-crib he swore he would not go any further to the rear. The squad moved on and left him standing there, pistol in hand, waiting for the enemy, who were now jumping the fences and coming across the field, running at the top of their speed. What became of this singular man no one knows. He was, as he said, "determined to make a stand." A little further on the squad found a single piece of artillery, manned by a lieutenant and two or three men. They were selecting individuals in the enemy's skirmish line, and *firing at them with solid shot!* Lieutenant McRae laughed at the ridiculous sight, remonstrated with the officer, and offered his squad to serve the gun, if there was any canister in the limber chest. The offer was refused, and again the squad moved on. Passing a cow-shed about this time, the squad halted to look with horror upon several dead and wounded Confederates who lay there upon the manure pile. They had suffered wounds and death upon this the last day of their country's struggle. Their wounds had received no attention, and those living were famished and burning with fever.

Lieutenant McRae, noticing a number of wagons and guns parked in a field near by, surprised at what he considered great carelessness in the immediate presence of the enemy, approached an officer on horseback and said, in his usual impressive manner, "I say there, what does this mean?" The man took his hand and quietly said, "We have surrendered." "I don't believe it, sir!" replied McRae, strutting around as mad as a hornet. "You mustn't talk so, sir! you will demoralize my men!" He was soon convinced, however, by seeing Yankee cavalrymen walking their horses around as composedly as though the Army of Northern Virginia had never existed. To say that McRae was surprised, disgusted, indignant, and incredulous, is a mild way of expressing his state of mind as he turned to his squad and said, "Well, boys, it must be so, *but it's very strange behavior*. Let's move on and see about it." As though dreaming, the squad and the disgusted officer moved on.

Learning that the army had gone into camp, the skirmishers went on in the direction of the village, and found the battalion in the woods near the main road. Fires were burning, and those who had been fortunate enough to find anything eatable were cooking. Federal troops were riding up and down the road and loafing about the camps trying to be familiar. They seemed to think that "How are you, Johnny?" spoken in condescending style, was sufficient introduction.

During the day a line of men came single file over the hill near the camp, each bearing on his shoulder a box of "hard-tack" or crackers. Behind these came a beef, driven by soldiers. The crackers and beef were a present from the Federal troops near, who, knowing the famishing condition of the surrounded army, had contributed their day's rations for its relief. All honor to them. It was a soldierly act which was thoroughly appreciated.

The beef was immediately shot and butchered, and before the animal heat had left the meat, it was impaled in little strips on sticks, bayonets, swords, and pocket-knives, and roasting over the fires.

Though numbers of the enemy visited the camps and plied the men with all sorts of questions, seeming very curious and inquisitive, not an unkind word was said on either side that day. When the skirmishers under McRae entered the camp of the battalion, their enthusiastic descriptions of driving the enemy and being driven in turn failed to produce any effect. Many of the men were sobbing and crying, like children recovering from convulsions of grief after a severe whipping. They were sorely grieved, mortified, and humiliated. Of course they had not the slightest conception of the numbers of the enemy who surrounded them.

Other men fairly raved with indignation, and declared their desire to escape or die in the attempt; but not a man was heard to blame General Lee. On the contrary, all expressed the greatest sympathy for him and declared their willingness to submit at once, or fight to the last man, as he ordered. At no period of the war was he held in higher veneration or regarded with more sincere affection, than on that sad and tearful day.

In the afternoon the little remnant of the army was massed in a field. General Gordon spoke to them most eloquently, and bade them farewell. General Walker addressed his division, to which Cutshaw's battalion was attached, bidding them farewell. In the course of his remarks he denounced fiercely the men who had thrown down their arms on the march, and called upon the true men before him to go home and tell their wives, mothers, sisters, and sweethearts how shamefully these cowards had behaved.

General Henry A. Wise also spoke, sitting on his horse and bending forward over the pommel of his saddle. Referring to the surrender, he said, " I would rather have embraced the tabernacle of death."

There were many heaving bosoms and tear-stained faces during the speaking. A tall, manly fellow, with his colors pressed to his side, stood near General Gordon, convulsed with grief.

The speaking over, the assembly dispersed, and once more the camp-fires burned brightly. Night brought long-needed rest. The heroes of many hard-fought battles, the conquerors of human nature's cravings, the brave old army, fell asleep — securely guarded by the encircling hosts of the enemy. Who will write the history of that march? Who will be able to tell the story? Alas! how many heroes fell!

The paroles, which were distributed on Tuesday, the 11th, were printed on paper about the size of an ordinary bank check, with blank spaces for the date, name of the prisoner, company, and regiment, and signature of the commandant of the company or regiment. They were signed by the Confederate officers themselves, and were as much respected by all picket officers, patrols, etc., of the Federal army as though they bore the signature of U. S. Grant. The following is a copy of one of these paroles, recently made from the original :

APPOMATTOX COURT HOUSE, VIRGINIA,
April 10, 1865.

The bearer, Private —— —— , of Second Company Howitzers, Cutshaw's Battalion, a paroled prisoner of the Army of Northern Virginia, has permission to go to his home and there remain undisturbed.

L. F. JONES,
Captain Commanding Second Company Howitzers.

The " guidon," or color-bearer, of the Howitzers had concealed the battle flag of the company about his person, and before the final separation cut it into pieces of about four by six inches, giving each man present a piece. Many of these scraps of faded silk are still preserved, and will be handed down to future generations. Captain Fry, who commanded after Colonel Cutshaw was wounded, assembled the battalion, thanked the men for their faithfulness, bid them farewell, and read the following : —

HEADQUARTERS ARMY NORTHERN VIRGINIA,
APPOMATTOX COURT HOUSE, *April* 10, 1865.

GENERAL ORDER NO. 9.

After four years of arduous service, marked by

unsurpassed courage and fortitude, the Army of Northern Virginia has been compelled to yield to overwhelming numbers and resources.

I need not tell the brave survivors of so many hard-fought battles, who have remained steadfast to the last, that I have consented to this result from no distrust of them; but feeling that valor and devotion could accomplish nothing that would compensate for the loss that must have attended a continuance of the contest, I determined to avoid the useless sacrifice of those whose past services have endeared them to their countrymen.

By the terms of agreement, officers and men can return to their homes and remain until exchanged. You will take with you the satisfaction that proceeds from the consciousness of duty faithfully performed, and I earnestly pray that a merciful God will extend to you his blessing and protection.

With an unceasing admiration of your constancy and devotion to your country, and a grateful remembrance of your kind and generous consideration for myself, I bid you all an affectionate farewell.

R. E. LEE.

This grand farewell from the man who had in the past personified the glory of his army and now bore its grief in his own great heart, was the signal for tearful partings. Comrades wept as they gazed upon each other, and with choking voices said, farewell! And so — they parted. Little groups of two or three or four, without food, without money, but with " the satisfaction that proceeds from the conscious- ness of duty faithfully performed," were soon plodding their way homeward.

CHAPTER IX

BITTER grief for the past, which seemed to be forever lost, and present humiliation, could not long suppress the anxious thought and question, "What now?" The discussion of the question brought relief from the horrid feeling of vacuity which oppressed the soldier and introduced him to the new sensations of liberty of choice, freedom of action — full responsibility. For capital he had a clear conscience, a brave heart, health, strength, and a good record. With these he sought his home.

Early in the morning of Wednesday, the 12th of April, without the stirring drum or the bugle call of old, the camp awoke to the new life. Whether or not they had a country these soldiers did not know. Home to many, when they reached it, was graves and ashes. At any rate there must be, somewhere on earth, a better place than a muddy, smoky camp in a piece of scrubby pines — better company than gloomy, hungry comrades and inquisitive enemies, and something in the future more exciting, if not more hopeful, than nothing to eat, nowhere to sleep, nothing to do, and nowhere to go. The disposition to start was apparent, and the preparations were promptly begun.

To roll up the old blanket and oil-cloth, gather up the haversack, canteen, axe, perhaps, and a few trifles, in time of peace of no value, eat the fragments that remained, and light a pipe, was the work of a few moments. This slight employment, coupled with pleasant anticipations of the unknown, and therefore possibly enjoyable future, served to restore somewhat the usual light-hearted manner of soldiers, and relieve the final farewells of much of their sadness. There was even a smack of hope and cheerfulness as the little groups sallied out into the world to combat they scarcely knew what. As we cannot follow all these groups, we will join ourselves to one and see them home.

Two " brothers - in - arms," whose objective point is Richmond, take the road on foot. They have nothing to eat and no money. They are bound for their home in a city, which, when they last heard from it, was in flames. What they will see when they arrive there they cannot imagine; but the instinctive love of home urges them. They walk on steadily and rapidly and are not diverted by surroundings. It does not even occur to them that their situation, surrounded on all sides by armed enemies and walking a road crowded with them, is at all novel. They are suddenly roused to a sense of their situation by a sharp " Halt! show your parole!" They had struck the cordon of picket posts which surrounded the surrendered army. It was the first exercise of authority by the Federal army. A sergeant, accompanied by a couple of muskets, stepped into the road, with a modest air examined the paroles and said quietly, " Pass on."

The strictly military part of the operation being over, the social commenced. As the two " survivors " moved on they were followed by numerous remarks, such as " Hello! Johnny, I say! going home?" " Ain't you glad!" They made no reply, these wayfarers, but they *thought* some very *emphatic remarks.*

From this point "On to Richmond!" was the grand thought. Steady work it was. The road, strangely enough considering the proximity of two armies, was quite lonesome, and not an incident of interest occurred during the day. Darkness found the two comrades still pushing on.

Some time after dark a light was seen a short distance ahead and there was a "sound of revelry." On approaching, the light was found to proceed from a large fire, built on the floor

11

of an old and dilapidated outhouse, and surrounded by a ragged, hungry, singing, and jolly
crowd of paroled prisoners of the Army of
Northern Virginia, who had gotten possession
of a quantity of corn meal and were waiting for
the ash-cakes then in the ashes. Being liberal,
they offered the new-comers some of their
bread. Being hungry, the " survivors " accepted — and eat their first meal that day.
Here seemed a good place to spend the night,
but the party in possession were so noisy, and
finally so quarrelsome and disagreeable generally, that the " survivors," after a short rest,
pushed on in the darkness, determined, if possible, to find some shelter more quiet. The result was a night march, which was continued
till the morning dawned.

Thursday morning they entered the village of
Buckingham Court House, and traded a small
pocket mirror for a substantial breakfast. There
was quite a crowd of soldiers gathered around
a cellar door, trying to persuade an ex-Confed-
erate A. A. A. Commissary of Subsistence that
he might as well, in view of the fact that the
army had surrendered, let them have some of
his stores ; and, after considerable persuasion
and some threats, he relinquished the hope of
keeping them for himself, and told the men to
help themselves. They did so.

The people of the village did not exactly doubt the *fact* of the surrender, but evidently thought matters had been *somewhat exaggerated*, facts suppressed, and everything allowed to fall into a very doubtful condition. Confederate money would not pass, however; *that* was settled *beyond doubt*.

As the two tramps were about to leave the village, and were hurrying along the high road which led through it, they saw a solitary horseman approaching from their rear. It was easy to recognize at once General Lee. He rode slowly, calmly along. As he passed an old tavern on the roadside, some ladies and children waved their handkerchiefs, smiled, and wept. The General turned his eyes to the porch on which they stood, and slowly putting his hand to his hat, raised it slightly, and as slowly again dropped his hand to his side. The survivors did not weep, but they had strange sensations. They pushed on, steering, so to speak, for Cartersville and the ferry.

Before leaving the village it was the sad duty of the survivors to stop at the humble abode of Mrs. P., and tell her of the death of her husband, who fell mortally wounded, pierced by a musket ball, near Sailor's Creek. She was also told that a comrade who was by his side when he fell, but who was not able to stay with him, would come along soon and give her the particulars. That comrade came and repeated the story. In a few days the "dead man" reached home alive and scarcely hurt. He was originally an infantryman, recently transferred to artillery, and therefore wore a small knapsack, as infantrymen did. The ball struck the knapsack with a "whack!" and knocked the man down. That was all.

Some time during the night the travelers reached the ferry at Cartersville. Darkness and silence prevailed there. Loud and continued shouts brought no ferryman, and eager searchings revealed no boat. The depth of the water being a thing unknown and not easily found out, it was obviously prudent to camp for the night.

On the river's edge there was an old building which seemed a brick one; one wall near the water's edge. A flight of steep, rough steps led to an open door on the second floor. Up these steps climbed the weary men. Inside there was absolute darkness, but there was shelter from the wind. Feeling about on the floor they satisfied themselves of its cleanliness and dryness. The faithful old blankets were once more spread, their owners laid down and at once fell into a deep sleep which was not broken till morning. The room was surpris-

ingly small. When the soldiers entered they
had no idea of the size of it, and went to sleep
with the impression that it was very large.
The morning revealed its dimensions — about
ten by twelve feet. The ferryman was early
at his post, and put the travelers across cheerfully without charge.

BUTTER MILK
AUNTY

Soon after crossing, a good silver-plated ta-
ble-spoon, bearing the monogram of one of
the travelers, purchased from an aged colored
woman a large chunk of ash-cake and about half
a gallon of buttermilk. This old darkey had
lived in Richmond in her younger days. She
spoke of grown men and women there as
"children whar I raised." "Lord! boss, does
you know Miss Sadie? Well, I nussed her and

I nussed all uv them chillun; that I did, sah!
Yawl chillun does look hawngry, that you does.
Well, you 's welcome to them vittles, and I 'm
powful glad to git dis spoon. God bless you,
honey ! " A big log on the roadside furnished
a seat for the comfortable consumption of the
before-mentioned ash-cake and milk. The feast
was hardly begun when the tramp of a horse's
hoofs was heard. Looking up the survivors
saw, with surprise, General Lee approaching.
He was entirely alone, and rode slowly along.
Unconscious that any one saw him, he was yet
erect, dignified, and apparently as calm and
peaceful as the fields and woods around him.
Having caught sight of the occupants of the
log, he kept his eyes fixed on them, and as he
passed, turned slightly, saluted, and said, in the
most gentle manner : " Good morning, gentlemen ; taking your breakfast ? " The soldiers
had only time to rise, salute, and say " Yes,
sir ! " and he was gone.

Having finished as far as they were able the
abundant meal furnished by the liberality of
the good " old mammy," the travelers resumed
their journey greatly refreshed.

It seems that General Lee pursued the road
which the survivors chose, and, starting later
than they, overtook them, he being mounted
and they on foot. At any rate, it was their

GOOD MORNING, GENTLEMEN.

good fortune to see him three times between Appomattox and Richmond. The incidents introducing General Lee are peculiarly interesting, and while the writer is in doubt as to the *day* on which the next and last incident occurred, the reader may rest assured of the truthfulness of the narration.

About the time when men who have eaten a hearty breakfast become again hungry — as good fortune would have it happen — the travellers reached a house pleasantly situated, and a comfortable place withal. Approaching the house they were met by an exceedingly kind, energetic, and hospitable woman. She promptly asked, " You are not deserters ? " " No," said the soldiers, " we have our paroles. We are from Richmond ; we are homeward bound, and called to ask if you could spare us a dinner ? " "Spare you a dinner ? certainly I can. My husband is a miller ; his mill is right across the road there, down the hill, and I have been cooking all day for the poor starving men. Take a seat on the porch there and I will get you something to eat." By the time the travelers were seated, this admirable woman was in the kitchen at work. The " pat-a-pat, pat, pat, pat, pat-a-pat-a-pat " of the sifter, and the cracking and " fizzing " of the fat bacon as it fried, saluted their hungry ears, and the delicious smell

tickled their olfactory nerves most delightfully.
Sitting thus, entertained by delightful sounds,
breathing the fragrant air, and wrapped in
meditation, — or anticipation rather, — the soldiers saw the dust rise in the air, and heard
the sound of an approaching party.

Several horsemen rode up to the road-gate,
threw their bridles over the posts or tied to the
overhanging boughs, and dismounted. They
were evidently officers, well dressed, fine looking
men, and about to enter the gate. Almost at
once the men on the porch recognized General
Lee and his son. An ambulance had arrived
at the gate also. Without delay the party entered and approached the house, General Lee
preceding the others. Satisfied that it was the
General's intention to enter the house, the two
" brave survivors " instinctively and respectfully, venerating the approaching man, determined to give him and his companions the
porch. As they were executing a rather rapid
and undignified flank movement to gain the
right and rear of the house, the voice of General Lee overhauled them, thus : " Where are
you men going ? " " This lady has offered to
give us a dinner, and we are waiting for it,"
replied the soldiers. " Well, you had better
move on now — this gentleman will have quite
a large party on him to-day," said the General.

The soldiers touched their caps, said "Yes, sir," and retired, somewhat hurt, to a strong position on a hencoop in the rear of the house. The party then settled on the porch.

The General had, of course, no authority, and the surrender of the porch was purely respectful. Knowing this the soldiers were at first hurt, but a moment's reflection satisfied them that the General was right. He *had suspicions of plunder*, and these were increased by the movement of the men to the rear as he approached. He *misinterpreted their conduct*.

The lady of the house (*a reward for her name!*) hearing the dialogue in the yard, pushed her head through the crack of the kitchen door, and, as she tossed a lump of dough from hand to hand and gazed eagerly out, addressed the soldiers: "Ain't that old General Lee?" "Yes; General Lee and his son and other officers come to dine with you," they replied. "Well," she said, "he ain't no better than the men that fought for him, and I don't reckon he is as hungry; so you just come in here. I am going to give you yours first, and then I'll get something for him!"

What a meal it was! Seated at the kitchen table, the large-hearted woman bustling about and talking away, the ravenous tramps attacked a pile of old Virginia hoe-cake and corn-dodger, a frying pan with an inch of gravy and slices of bacon, streak of lean and streak of fat, very numerous.   To finish — as much rich butter-milk as the drinkers could contain. With many heartfelt thanks the survivors bid farewell to this immortal woman, and leaving the General and his party in quiet possession of the front porch, pursued their way.

Night found the survivors at the gate of a quite handsome, framed, country residence. The weather was threatening, and it was desirable to have shelter as well as rest.   Entering, and knocking at the door, they were met by a ser-vant girl.   She was sent to her mistress with a request for permission to sleep on her premises. The servant returned, saying, " Mistis say she 's a widder, and there ain't no gentleman in the house, and she can't let you come in."   She was sent with a second message, which informed the lady that the visitors were from Richmond, members of a certain company from there, and would be content to sleep on the porch, in the stable, or in the barn.   They would protect her property, etc., etc., etc.

This brought the lady of the house to the door.   She said, " If you are members of the —— ——, you must know my nephew; he was in that company."   Of course they knew him.   " Old chum," " Comrade," " Particular friend," "Splendid fellow," "Hope he was well when you heard from him. Glad to meet you, madam!" These and similar hearty expressions brought the longed for "Come in, gentlemen; you are welcome. I will see that supper is prepared for you at once." (Invitation accepted.)

The old haversacks were deposited in a corner under the steps, and their owners conducted down-stairs to a spacious dining-room, quite prettily furnished. A large table occupied the centre of the room, and at one side there was a handsome display of silver in a glass-front case. A good big fire lighted the room. The lady sat quietly working at some woman's work, and from time to time questioning, in a *rather suspicious* manner, her guests. Their correct answers satisfied her, and their respectful manner reassured her, so that by the time supper was brought in she was chatting and laughing with her " defenders."

The supper came in steaming hot. It was abundant, well prepared, and served elegantly. Splendid coffee, hot biscuit, luscious butter, fried ham, eggs, fresh milk! The writer could not expect to be believed if he should tell the quantity eaten at that meal. The good lady of the house enjoyed the sight. She relished every mouthful, and no doubt realized then and there the blessing which is conferred on hospitality, and the truth of that saying of old: " It is more blessed to give than to receive."

The wayfarers were finally shown to a neat little chamber. The bed was soft and glistening white. Too white and clean to be soiled by the occupancy of two Confederate soldiers who had not had a change of underclothing for many weeks. They looked at it, felt of it, spread their old blankets on the neat carpet, and slept there till near the break of day.

While it was yet dark the travelers, unwilling to lose time waiting for breakfast, crept out of the house, leaving their thanks for their kind hostess, and pressed rapidly on to Manikin Town, on the James River and Kanawha Canal, half a day's march from Richmond, where they arrived while it was yet early morning. The green sward between the canal and river was inviting, and the survivors laid there awhile to rest and determine whether or not they would push on to the city. They decided to do so as soon as they could find a breakfast to fit them for the day's march.

A short walk placed them at the yard gate of a house prominent by reason of its size and finish. Everything indicated comfort, plenty, and freedom from the ravages of war. The proprietor, a well-fed, hearty man, of not more than

forty-two or three, who, as a soldier could tell
at a glance, had never seen a day's service,
stood behind the tall gate, and, without a motion towards opening it, replied to the cheery
" Good morning, sir," of the soldiers with a
sullen " morn ; what do you want here ? " " We
are from Richmond, sir, members of the ——
——. We are on our way home from Appomattox, where the army was surrendered, and
called to ask if you could spare us something to
eat before we start on the day's march." " Oh,
yes ! *I* know about the surrender, *I* do. Some
scoundrels were here last night and stole my
best mare, d—— 'em ! No, I don't want any
more of such cattle here," replied the patriot.
(A *large* reward for *his* name.) The foragers,
having worked for a meal before and being less
sensitive than " penniless gentlemen " sometimes
are, replied, " *We* are not horse-thieves or beg-
gars. If you do not feel that it would be a
pleasure and a privilege to feed us, *don't do it.*
We don't propose to press the matter."

At last he said, " Come in, then ; I 'll see
what I can do." The seekers after food accepted the ungracious invitation, followed the
dog through his yard and into his house, and
took seats at his table. At a signal from the
master a servant went out. The host followed, and, it is supposed, instructed her. The

host returned, and was soon followed by the
servant bearing two plates, which were placed
before the survivors. Alas! that they should
"survive" to see that the plates contained the
heads, tails, fins, and vertebræ of the fish, fresh
from the river, which the family of this hero
and sufferer from the evils of war had devoured
at their early, and, no doubt, cozy breakfast.

Survivor No. 1 looked at Survivor No. 2,
Survivor No. 2 looked at Survivor No. 1, and
simultaneously they rose to their feet, glanced
at the "host," and strode to and out of the
door. The "host" followed, amazed. "What's
the matter, gentlemen? You did not eat."
The "poor soldiers" replied: "No, we did n't
eat; we are not dogs. Permit us to say we are
satisfied it would be an injustice to the canine
race to call *you* one. You deserve to lose another mare. You are meaner than any epithets at our command."

The man fairly trembled. His face was pale
with rage, but he dared not reply as he would.
Recovering himself, and seeing an "odorous"
name in the future, he attempted apology and
reparation for the insult, and complete reconcil-
iation. "Oh, come in, come in! I'll have
something cooked for you. Sorry the mistake
occurred. All right, all right, boys; come in,"
pulling and patting the "boys." But the boys

would n't "go in." On the contrary, they
stayed out persistently, and, before they left
that gate, heaped on its owner all the contempt,
disdain, and scorn which they could express;
flung at him all the derisive epithets which four
years in the army places at a man's disposal;
pooh poohed at his hypocritical regrets; and
shaking off the dust of that place from their
feet, pushed on to the city, the smoke of which
rose to heaven.

At eleven A. M. of the same day, two footsore, despondent, and penniless men stood facing
the ruins of the home of a comrade who had
sent a message to his mother. " Tell mother
I am coming." The ruins yet smoked. A relative of the lady whose home was in ashes, and
whose son said "I am coming," stood by the
survivors. " Well, then," he said, " it must be
true that General Lee has surrendered." The
solemnity of the remark, coupled with the certainty in the minds of the survivors, was almost
amusing. The relative pointed out the temporary residence of the mother, and thither the
survivors wended their way.

A knock at the door startled the mother, and,
with agony in her eyes, she appeared at the
open door, exclaiming, "My poor boys!" —
" Are safe, and coming home," said the survivors. " Thank God!" said the mother, and the
tears flowed down her cheeks.

A rapid walk through ruined and smoking streets, some narrow escapes from negro soldiers on police duty, the satisfaction of seeing two of the "boys in blue" hung up by their thumbs for pillaging, a few handshakings, and the survivors found their way to the house of a relative where they did eat bread with thanks.

A friend informed the survivors that farm hands were needed all around the city. They made a note of the name of one farmer. Saturday night the old blankets were spread on the parlor floor. Sunday morning, the 16th of April, they bid farewell to the household, and started for the farmer's house.

As they were about to start away, the head of the family took from his pocket a handful of odd silver pieces, and extending it to his guests, told them it was all he had, but they were *welcome to half of it!* Remembering that he had a wife and three or four children to feed, the soldiers smiled through *their* tears at his, bade him keep it all, and "weep for himself rather than for them." So saying, they departed, and at sundown were at the farmer's house, fourteen miles away. Monday morning, the 17th, they "beat their swords" (muskets, in this case) into plow-shares, and did the first day's work of the *sixty* which the simple farmer secured at a cost to himself of about *half rations* for two men. Behold the gratitude of a people!

CHAPTER X.

SUNDAY night, April 16th, the two survivors sat down to a cozy supper at the farmer's house. Plentiful it was, and, to hungry travelers, sweet and satisfying. The presence of the farmer's wife and children, two lady refugees, and an old gentleman, who was also a refugee, added greatly to the novelty and pleasure of the meal.

After supper the soldiers were plied with questions till they were almost overcome by fatigue and about to fall asleep in their chairs.

At last the farmer, with many apologies, led them kindly to the best room in the house, the parlor, where they spread their blankets on the carpeted floor and were soon sound asleep.

In the morning the breakfast was enough to craze a Confederate soldier. Buttermilk-biscuit, fresh butter, eggs, milk, fried bacon, coffee! After the breakfast, business.

The farmer proposed to feed and lodge the soldiers, and pay them eleven dollars monthly, for such manual labor as they could perform on his farm. The soldiers, having in remembrance the supper and breakfast, accepted the terms. The new "hands" were now led to the garden, where the farmer had half an acre plowed up, and each was furnished with an old, dull hoe, with crooked, knotty handles. The farmer then, with blushes and stammering, explained that he desired to have each particular clod chopped up fine with the hoe. The soldiers — town men — thought this an almost superhuman task and a great waste of time, but, so that the work procured food, they cared not what the work might be, and at it they went with a will. All that morning, until the dinner hour, those two hoes rose and fell as regularly as the pendulum of a clock swings from side to side, and almost as fast.

The negro men and women in the neighborhood, now in the full enjoyment of newly-conferred liberty, and consequently having no thought of doing any work, congregated about the garden, leaned on the fence, gazed sleepily at the toiling soldiers, chuckled now and then, and occasionally explained their presence by remarking to each other, "Come here to see dem dar white folks wuckin."

There were onions growing in that garden, which the soldiers were glad to pull up and eat. It was angel's food to men who had fed for

SEE DEM WHITE FOLKS WUCKIN

months on salt bacon and corn bread without one mouthful of any green thing. When dinner time came the "hands" were, to say the least, very decidedly hungry.

Buttermilk-biscuit figured prominently again, and the soldiers found great difficulty in exercising any deliberation in the eating of them. It really seemed to them that, were it reasonable behavior, they could devour every morsel provided for the entire family. But when they had devoured about two thirds of all there was to eat, and the host said, " Have another biscuit?" they replied, " No, thank you, *plenty* — greatest plenty!" all the while as hungry as when they sat down. It was only a question of *who* was to be hungry — the soldiers or the children. There was not enough for all. After dinner the survivors went again to the garden and chopped those clods of earth until the merry voice of the farmer called them to supper.

At supper there was a profusion of flowers which, the kind lady of the house explained, were there to cheer the soldiers. She had noticed they were sad, and hoped that this little attention would cheer them. But the thing the soldiers most needed to enliven them was more to eat. They were not feeling romantic at all.

After the supper the whole family adjourned

to the parlor and were entertained with some good old-fashioned piano playing and homespun duets and solos. The veterans added their mite to the entertainment in the shape of a tolerably fair tenor and an intolerable bass. Singing in the open air, with a male chorus, is not the best preparation for a parlor mixed quartette.

When the war ceased the negroes on the farm had left their quarters and gone out in search of a glorious something which they had heard described as "liberty," freedom, "manhood," and the like. Consequently the "quarters" suggested themselves to the farmer as a good place for the new field hands to occupy for sleeping apartments. They were carried to an out-building and shown their room, ten by fifteen feet, unplastered, greasy, and dusty. The odor of the "man and brother" did cling there still. A bench, a stool, an old rickety bedstead, and a bed of straw, completed the fitting out of the room. Save for the shelter of the roof, anywhere in the fields would have been far preferable. The first night disclosed the presence of fleas in abundance, and other things worse.

While it was yet dark the farmer, still somewhat embarrassed by the possession of the new style of laborer, began to call, " Time to get up bo — gentlemen ! " " Hallo there ! " bang, bang, bang ! After a while the new hands appeared outside, and as they looked around noticed that the sun was looking larger and redder than they remembered it and too low down. The morning air was chilling, and grass, bushes, everything, dripping with dew.

The farmer led the way to the stable yard, and pointing to a very lively, restless, muscular young bull with handsome horns and glaring eyes, said he was to be yoked and hitched to the cart. If he had asked them to bridle and saddle an untamed African lion they would not have been more unwilling or less competent. So the farmer, telling them the animal was very gentle and harmless, proceeded to yoke and hitch him, hoping, he said, that having once seen the operation, his new hands would know how. The yoke was a sort of collar, and when the hitching was done the bull stood in the shafts of the cart just as a horse would. Instead of a bridle and reins a heavy iron chain with links an inch and a half long was passed around the base of the animal's horns. The driver held the end of the chain and managed the animal by giving it tremendous jerks, which never failed to thrill the bull with agony, if one might judge from the expression of his countenance and the eagerness with which he rammed

his horns into pine-trees, or anything near,
whenever he felt the shock. The soldiers constantly marveled that his horns did not drop
off. But they were not familiar with country
life, and especially ignorant of the art of driving
an ox-cart.

After breakfast the younger of the two survivors was told to take the cart, drawn by the
animal already described, and go down into the
woods after a load of cord-wood for the kitchen
fire. The trip *to* the woods was comparatively

Bull Team

easy. The wood was soon loaded on the cart,
and the journey home commenced. After going a few yards the animal concluded to stop.
His driver, finding that coaxing would not induce him to start, slacked the chain, gave it a
quick, strong jerk, and started him. He went
off at a fearful rate, with his nose on the ground
and his tail flying like a banner in the air. In

a moment he managed to hang a sapling which halted him, but summoning all his strength for a great effort, he bent himself to the yoke, the sapling slowly bent forward, and the axle mounted it. In another moment the sapling had righted itself, but the cart was turned over completely, and the wood on the ground. There were a great many mosquitoes, gnats, and flies in those woods, and they were biting furiously. Possibly that may account for the exasperated condition of the driver and his use of strong expressions there.

The cart was righted, the wood piled on again, and, strange to say, got out of the woods without further mishap. But in order to reach the house it was necessary to drive up the slope of a hill-side, with here and there a stump. On the way up the driver saw a stump ahead and determined to avoid it. So he gave the chain a shake. But the animal preferred to " straddle " the stump, and would have succeeded but for the fact that it was too high to pass beneath the axle. As soon as he felt the resistance of the stump against the axle, he made splendid exertions to overcome it, and succeeded in walking off with the body of the cart, leaving the axle and wheels behind. He did n't go far, however. The farmer came down and re-leased the weary animal. The survivor then "toted" the wood, stick by stick, to the house, and learned thereby the value of cord-wood ready to hand. People who are raised in the country have simple ways, but they can do some things much better than town-people can. They are useful people. They are not afraid of cattle or horses. The next day this awful animal was yoked to a plow and placed under the care of the elder of the survivors, who was to plow a field near the house. In a few minutes he did something displeasing to the bull, which started him to running at a fearful speed. He dashed away towards the house, the plow flying and flapping about like the arms of a flail; tore through the flower-beds, ripping them to pieces; tore down all the choice young trees about the house; frightened the ladies and children nearly to death, and demoralized the whole farm. He was at last captured and affectionately cared for by the farmer, who, no doubt, felt that it was a pity for any man to be compelled to trust his valuable stock to the management of green hands.

In the mean time the "other man" had been furnished with a harrow and a mule and sent to harrow a field. The farmer pointed, carelessly no doubt, to a field and said, "Now you go there and drag that field. You know how, don't you? Well!" So he went and dragged that old harrow up and down, up and down, for many a weary hour. Towards dinner time he heard a voice in the distance, as of some one in distress. "Heigh! Ho-o-o-o! Say there! Stop! Sto-o-o-o-op! Hold on!"

There came the farmer running, panting, gesticulating, and screaming. Standing in astonishment the agricultural survivor awaited his arrival and an explanation of his strange conduct. As soon as the farmer had breath to speak he said, "Ah, me! Oh my! Mister, my dear sir! You have gone sir, and sir, you have tore up *all my turnip salad!*" And he wept there sorely. You see the farmer pointed out the field carelessly, and the "hand" got on the *wrong* one. He noticed some vegetation shooting up here and there, but supposed it was some weed the farmer wished to eradicate. Town-people don't know everything, and soldiers *are so careless.*

The three refugees before mentioned were an old gentleman, his aged wife, and their widowed daughter. Having lost their home and all their worldly possessions, they had agreed to work for the farmer for food and lodging. The old gentleman was acting somewhat in the character of coachman; his wife was nurse; and the widowed daughter was cook and house-servant. The three were fully the equals if not the supe-

riors of the family in which they were serving.
Happily for them they soon got some good
news, and drove away in their own carriage.
The farmer did the best he could for them
while they stayed, and for his survivors; but
he was burdened with a large family, a mis-
erably poor farm, deep poverty, and hopeless
shiftlessness.

One day the farmer made up his mind to cul-
tivate a certain field, in the centre of which he
had an extensive cow-pen, inclosed by a ten-
rail fence.   To prepare the way he wanted that
fence taken down, carried rail by rail to the
corner of the field, and there piled up.   He put
one of his new hands to work at this interesting job, and went home, probably to take a nap.
The survivor toted rails that day on one shoulder until it was bleeding, and then on the other
until that was too sensitive.   Then he walked
over to see how the other " hand " was getting
along with the horse and mule team and the
harrow.

He found him very warm, very much exasperated, using excited language, beating the
animals, and declaring that no man under the
sun ever encountered such formidable difficulties in the pursuit of agricultural profit.   He
explained that the horse was too large and the
mule too small; the traces were too old, and

would break every few yards; the harness was dropping to pieces; the teeth constantly dropping out of the harrow; and the harrow itself ready to tumble into firewood. In addition to these annoyances, the mule and the horse alternated between going the wrong way and not going at all. The man almost wept as he described the aggravating calmness of the animals. When a trace broke they turned, gazed on the wreck, stood still, groaned (by way of a sigh), and seemed to say, " One more brief respite, thank Providence! Fifteen minutes to tie up that old chain, *at least!*" After a careful survey of the situation and some tolerably accurate guesses as to the proximity of the dinner hour, the two battered remnants of the glorious old army decided to suspend operations, and slowly wended their way to the house: one carrying his lacerated shoulders, and the other steering the remains of the harrow.

It had been agreed — indeed, the " remnants " had insisted — that they were to be directed about their work and made to serve exactly as the negro hands would have been had they remained. But, so novel was the situation, the farmer had constantly to be reminded of his authority. At last a bright idea occurred to the farmer. He would undertake a little extra-fine work for a neighbor, and thus relieve the survivors of the monotony of the hoe, the plow, and the harrow. Some old ladies wanted their household goods moved from one house to another, and we were to undertake the job.

The entire force consisted of the mule and the cart thereto belonging, and the bull and his cart. The mule had precedence in the line, and was closely followed by the bull. The farmer walked in front as pioneer, the elder survivor drove the mule, and the hero of the cow-pen held the chain which agonized the bull when necessary.

At the brow of a certain long hill, which the humble mule had quietly walked down, the bull halted for meditation. His impatient and less romantic driver thoughtlessly gave the chain a rude jerk. In an instant he felt himself whirled down that hill at breakneck speed. Almost simultaneous with the start was the shock of the stop. Picking himself up, the driver found his cart securely fastened to a pine-tree, which was jammed between the wheel and the body of it. The steed was unhurt, but excited. After a long coaxing the farmer persuaded him to back far enough to disengage the cart, and the progress continued.

The furniture was found in a small room, up a crooked and narrow stairs. Nothing was as large as the furniture. How to get it out was

a conundrum.   One of the survivors suggested
to the farmer to knock off the roof of the house,
and take it out that way.   But he wouldn't
hear of it.   Finally, the cart was driven under
the eaves, and while " those whose past services
had endeared them to their countrymen " rolled
the furniture out of the window and lowered it
" by hand " from the eaves, the farmer stowed
it in the cart.   The ladies, though greatly agi-
tated by the imminent danger of the furniture,
found time to admire the ingenuity and origi-
nality of the plan and the intrepid daring of its
execution.   The farmer, who had several times
been in danger of having himself mashed flat,
was entirely overlooked.   Both the carts being
loaded, the train moved off in good order.

After a few days the farmer mounted one of
the men, " not conquered, but wearied with victory," on the mule, gave him an old meal-bag,
and sent him to a neighbor's for meal and bacon.   He got, say, a peck of one and a pound
or two of the other.   This proceeding was repeated at intervals of a day or two, and finally
led to the conclusion that the farmer was living
from hand to mouth certainly, and in all probability on charity.   Besides, the " new hands "
felt a growing indisposition, owing to the mea-
gre supplies on the table, to allow themselves
any latitude in the matter of eating.   So they

resolved to try the good old plan of days gone by, and send out a foraging party. The plans were discussed at length, and everything decided.

One morning, early, the senior of the "endeared" survivors took the road for Richmond, distant about fourteen miles, intending there to lay in food, tobacco, pipes, information, and any other little thing calculated to brighten life on a farm. During his absence the other forlorn survivor groaned with impatience and doubt, questioning the possibility of a man returning to such a place after seeing the luxurious supplies of good eating on exhibition by the Yankee sutlers in Richmond.

But he did return, like a good comrade, bringing his "plunder" with him. He made the round trip of twenty-eight miles on foot, and at midnight reached the "quarters" with cold ham, good bread, pipes, smoking tobacco, chewing tobacco, a few clean clothes, and a good pair of shoes, which one of the party needed. These were the gift of an old friend in town. Sitting on the bedside, as morning approached, they made a hearty meal, and then smoked, smoked, smoked, as only men can smoke who love to smoke and have not had the wherewithal for a week or two.

The returned forager told of the strange

sights he had seen in town. Some young Confederates, who were smart, were at work in the ruins cleaning bricks at five dollars a day. Others had government work, as clerks, mechanics, and laborers, earning from one to five dollars a day. The government had established commissary stores at different points in the city, where rations were sold, at nominal prices, to those who could buy, and supplied gratis to those who could not. He had seen gray-haired old gentlemen, all their lives used to plenty, standing about these places, waiting "their turn" to "draw." Soldiers marched by twos and fours and by companies, everywhere. Captains and lieutenants, sergeants and corporals, were the masters of the city and a sort of temporary Providence, dictating what sort of clothes the people were to wear, what they might eat, what they might do, what they might say and think; in short, allowing the people to live, as it were, on a "limited" ticket.

But among other things the forager brought information to the effect that he had secured employment for both at the cheering rate of five dollars per week.

So one day these two " laid down the shovel and the hoe," and made most excellent time for Richmond, arriving there early in the day, and entering at once upon the new work.

During the stay at the farm the survivors felt that they were not yet returned to civil life, but " foraging " on the neutral ground between war and peace, — neither soldiers nor citizens. But now, in regular employment, in a city, —

C.S. Buttons off

their own city! — with so much per week and the responsibility of " finding themselves," and especially after the provost made them cut the brass buttons off their jackets, and more especially after they were informed that they must take the oath before doing anything else, they began to think that probably the war was nearing its end. But a real good hearty war like that dies hard. No country likes to part with a good earnest war. It likes to talk about the war, write its history, fight its battles over and over again, and build monument after monument to commemorate its glories.

A long time after a war, people begin to find out, as they read, that the deadly struggle marked a grand period in their history!

13

CHAPTER XI.

THE soldier may forget the long, weary
march, with its dust, heat, and thirst, and he
may forget the horrors and blood of the battle-
field, or he may recall them sadly, as he thinks
of the loved dead; but the cheerful, happy
scenes of the camp-fire he will never forget.
How willingly he closes his eyes to the present
to dream of those happy, careless days and
nights! Around the fire crystallize the memories of the soldier's life. It was his home,
his place of rest, where he met with good com-
panionship. *Who kindled the fire?* Nobody
had matches, there was no fire in sight, and yet
scarcely was the camp determined when the
bright blaze of the camp-fire was seen. *He* was
a shadowy fellow who kindled the fire. Nobody
knows who he was; but no matter how wet the
leaves, how sobby the twigs, no matter if there
was no fire in a mile of the camp, that fellow
could start one. Some men might get down on
hands and knees, and blow it and fan it, rear
and charge, and fume and fret, and yet " she

would n't burn." But this fellow would come, kick it all around, scatter it, rake it together again, shake it up a little, and oh, *how it burned!* The little flames would bite the twigs and snap at the branches, embrace the logs, and leap and dance and laugh, at the touch of the master's hand, and soon lay at his feet a bed of glowing coals.

As soon as the fire is kindled all hands want water. Who can find it? Where is it? Never mind; we have a man who knows where to go. He says, " Where 's our bucket? " and then we hear the rattle of the old tin cup as it drops to the bottom of it, and away he goes, nobody knows where. But *he* knows, and he does n't stop to think, but without the slightest hesitation or doubt strikes out in the darkness. From the camp-fire as a centre, draw 500 radii, and start an ordinary man on any of them, and let him walk a mile on each, and he will miss the water. But that fellow in the mess with the water instinct never failed. He would go as straight for the spring, or well, or creek, or river, as though he had lived in that immediate neighborhood all his life and never got water anywhere else. What a valuable man he was! A modest fellow, who never knew his own greatness. But others remember and honor him. May he never want for any good thing!

Having a roaring fire and a bucket of good water, we settle down. A man cannot be comfortable " *anywhere;* " so each man and his " chum " picks out a tree, and that particular tree becomes the homestead of the two. They hang their canteens on it, lay their haversacks and spread their blankets at the foot of it, and sit down and lean their weary backs against it, and feel that they are at home. How gloomy the woods are beyond the glow of our fire! How cozy and comfortable we are who stand around it and inhale the aroma of the coffee-boiler and skillet!

The man squatting by the fire is a person of importance. He does n't talk, not he ; his whole mind is concentrated on that skillet. He is our cook, — volunteer, natural and talented cook. Not in a vulgar sense. He does n't mix, but simply bakes, the biscuit. Every faculty, all the energy, of the man is employed in that great work. Don't suggest anything to him if you value his friendship. Don't attempt to put on or take off from the top of that skillet one single coal, and don't be in a hurry for the biscuit. You need not say you " like yours half done," etc. Simply wait. When he thinks they are ready, and not before, you get them. *He* may raise the lid cautiously now and then and look in, but don't *you* look in.

Don't say you think they are done, because it's useless.   Ah! his face relaxes; he raises the lid, turns it upside down to throw off the coals, and says, *All right, boys!* And now, with the air of a wealthy philanthropist, he distributes the solid and weighty product of his skill to, as it were, the humble dependents around him.

The " General" of the mess, having satisfied the cravings of the inner man, now proceeds to enlighten the ordinary members of it as to when, how, and why, and where, the campaign will open, and what will be the result.   He arranges for every possible and impossible contingency, and brings the war to a favorable and early termination.   The greatest mistake General Lee ever made was that he failed to consult this man.   Who can tell what " might have been " if he had?

Now, to the consternation of all hands, our old friend " the Bore," familiarly known as " the old Auger," opens his mouth to tell us of a little incident illustrative of his personal prowess, and, by way of preface, commences at Eden, and goes laboriously through the patriarchal age, on through the Mosaic dispensation, to the Christian era, takes in Grecian and Roman history by the way, then Spain and Germany and England and colonial times, and the early history of our grand republic, the causes of and necessity for our war, and a complete history up to date, and then slowly unfolds the little matter. We always loved to hear this man, and prided ourselves on being the only mess in the army having such treasure *all our own.*

The "Auger," having been detailed for guard-duty, walks off ; his voice grows fainter and fainter in the distance, and we call forth our poet. One eye is bandaged with a dirty cotton rag. He is bare-headed, and his hair resembles a dismantled straw stack. His elbows and knees are out, and his pants, from the knee down, have a brown-toasted tinge imparted by the genial heat of many a fire. His toes protrude themselves prominently from his shoes. You would say, "What a dirty, ignorant fellow." But listen to his rich, well-modulated voice. How perfect his memory ! What graceful gestures ! How his single eye glows ! See the color on his cheek ! See the strained and still attention of the little group around him as he steps into the light of the fire ! Hear him !

> "I am dying, Egypt, dying !
>   Ebbs the crimson life-tide fast,
> And the dark Plutonian shadows
>   Gather on the evening blast.
> Let thine arms, O Queen, support me,
>   Hush thy sobs and bow thine ear ;
> Listen to the great heart secrets —
>   Thou, and thou alone, must hear.

THE POET OF OUR MESS.

.   .   .   .

"I am dying, Egypt, dying!
    Hark! the insulting foeman's cry.
  They are coming! quick! my falchion!!
    Let me front them ere I die.
  Ah! no more amid the battle
    Shall my heart exulting swell —
  Isis and Osiris guard thee —
    Cleopatra! Rome! Farewell!"

"Good!" "Bully!" "Go ahead, Jack!"
"Give us some more, old fellow!" And he
generally did, much to everybody's satisfaction.
We all loved Jack, *the Poet* of our mess. He
sleeps, his battles o'er, in Hollywood.

The *Singing* man generally put in towards
the last, and sung us to bed. He was generally
a diminutive man, with a sweet voice and a
sweetheart at home. His songs had in them
rosy lips, blue eyes, golden hair, pearly teeth,
and all that sort of thing. Of course he would
sing some good rollicking songs, in order to give
all a chance. And so, with hearty chorus,
"Three times around went she," "Virginia,
Virginia, the Land of the Free," "No surrender," "Lula, Lula, Lula is gone," "John Brown's
Body," with many variations, "Dixie," "The
Bonny Blue Flag," "Farewell to the Star-Span-
gled Banner," "Hail Columbia," with immense
variations, and "Maryland, My Maryland," till
about the third year of the war, when we be-

gan to think Maryland had "breathed and
burned" long enough, and ought to "come."
What part of her did come was *first-class*.
How the woods did ring with song! There
were patriotic songs, romantic and love songs,
sarcastic, comic, and war songs, pirates' glees,
plantation melodies, lullabies, good old hymn
tunes, anthems, Sunday-school songs, and everything but vulgar and obscene songs; these were
scarcely ever heard, and were nowhere in the
army well received or encouraged.

The recruit — our latest acquisition — was
so interesting. His nice clean clothes, new hat,
new shoes, trimming on his shirt front, letters
and cross-guns on his hat, new knife for all the
fellows to borrow, nice comb for general use,
nice little glass to shave by, good smoking tobacco, money in his pocket to lend out, oh,
what a great convenience he was! How *many*
things he had that a fellow could borrow, and
how willing he was to go on guard, and get wet,
and give away his rations, and bring water, and
cut wood, and ride horses to water! And he was
so clean and sweet, and his cheeks so rosy, all
the fellows wanted to bunk with him under his
nice new blanket, and impart to him some of
their numerous and energetic "tormentors."

And then it was so *interesting* to hear him
talk. He knew *so much* about war, arms, tents,

knapsacks, ammunition, marching, fighting, camping, cooking, shooting, and everything a soldier is and does. It is remarkable how much a recruit and how little an old soldier knows about such things. After a while the recruit forgets all, and is as ignorant as any veteran. How good the fellows were to a really gentlemanly boy! How they loved him!

The *Scribe* was a wonderful fellow and very useful. He could write a two-hours' pass, sign the captain's name better than the captain himself, and endorse it "respectfully forwarded approved," sign the colonel's name after "respectfully forwarded approved," and then on up to the commanding officer. And do it so well! Nobody wanted anything better. The boys had great veneration for the scribe, and used him constantly.

The *Mischievous* man was very useful. He made fun. He knew how to volunteer to shave a fellow with a big beard and moustache. He wouldn't lend his razor, but he'd shave him very well. He shaves one cheek, one half the chin, one side of the upper lip, puts his razor in his pocket, walks off, and leaves his customer the most one-sided chap in the army. He knew how to do something like this *every day*. What a treasure to a mess!

The *Forager* was a good fellow. He always

divided with the mess. If there was butter-
milk anywhere inside of ten miles he found it.
Apples he could smell from afar off. If any-
body was killing pork in the county he got the
spare-ribs. If a man had a cider cart on the

road he saw him first and bought him out. No
hound had a keener scent, no eagle a sharper
eye. How indefatigable he was! Distance,
rivers, mountains, pickets, patrols, roll-calls, —
nothing could stop or hinder him. He never
bragged about his exploits; simply brought in
the spoils, laid them down, and said, "Pitch in."

Not a word of the weary miles he had traveled,
how he begged or how much he paid, — simply
"Pitch in."

The *Commissary* man — he happened to be
in our mess — never had any sugar over, any
salt, any soda, any coffee — oh, no! But beg
him, plead with him, bear with him when he
says, "Go way, boy! Am I the commissary-
general? Have I got all the sugar in the Confederacy? Don't you know rations are short
now?" Then see him relax. "Come here,
my son; untie that bag there, and look in that
old jacket, and you will find another bag, — a
little bag, — and look in there and you will find
some sugar. Now go round and tell everybody
in camp, won't you. Tell 'em all to come and
get some sugar. *Oh! I know you won't. Oh
yes, of course!*"

As a general rule every mess had a "Bully"
and an "Argument man." Time would fail me
to tell of the "lazy man," the "brave man,"
the "worthless man," the "ingenious man,"
the "helpless man," the "sensitive man," and
the "gentleman," but they are as familiar to
the members of the mess as the "honest man,"
who would not eat stolen pig, but would "take
a little of the gravy."

Every soldier remembers — indeed, was per-
sonally acquainted with — the *Universal* man.

How he denied vehemently his own identity, and talked about " poison oak," and heat, and itch, and all those things, and strove, in the presence of those who knew how it was themselves, to prove his absolute freedom from anything like " universality ! " Poor fellow ! sulphur internally and externally would not do. Alas ! his only hope was to acknowledge his unhappy state, and stand, in the presence of his peers, confessed.

The " Boys in Blue " generally preferred to camp in the open fields. The Confeds took to the woods, and so the Confederate camp was not as orderly or as systematically arranged, but the most picturesque of the two. The blazing fire lit up the forms and faces and trees around it with a ruddy glow, but only deepened the gloom of the surrounding woods ; so that the soldier pitied the poor fellows away off on guard in the darkness, and, hugging himself, felt how good it was to be with the fellows around the fire. How companionable was the blaze and the glow of the coals ! They warmed the heart as well as the foot. The imagination seemed to feed on the glowing coals and surrounding gloom, and when the soldier gazed on the fire peace, liberty, home, strolls in the woods and streets with friends, the church, the school, playmates, and sweethearts all passed

before him, and even the dead came to mind.
Sadly, yet pleasantly, he thought of the loved
and lost; the future loomed up, and the possibility of death and prison and the grief at
home would stir his heart, and the tears would
fall trickling to the ground.   Then was the time
to fondle the little gifts from home; simple
things, — the little pin-cushion, the needle-case,
with thread and buttons, the embroidered tobacco bag, and the knitted gloves.   Then the
time to gaze on photographs, and to read and
re-read the letter telling of the struggles at
home, and the coming box of good things, —
butter and bread, toasted and ground coffee,
sugar cakes and pies, and other comfortable
things, prepared, by self-denial, for the soldier,
brother, and son.   Then the time to call on God
to spare, protect, and bless the dear, defenseless,
helpless ones at home.   Then the time for high
resolves; to read to himself his duty; to "re-
enlist for the war."   Then his heart grew to
his comrades, his general, and his country; and
as the trees, swept by the wintry winds, moaned
around him, the soldier slept and dreamed, and
dreamed of home, sweet home.

Those whose knowledge of war and its effects on the character of the soldier was gleaned
from the history of the wars of Europe and of
ancient times, greatly dreaded the demoraliza-

tion which they supposed would result from the
Confederate war for independence, and their
solicitude was directed mainly towards the
young men of Virginia and the South who were
to compose the armies of the Confederate
States. It was feared by many that the biv-
ouac, the camp-fires, and the march would ac-
custom the ears of their bright and innocent
boys to obscenity, oaths, and blasphemy, and
forever destroy that purity of mind and soul
which was their priceless possession when they
bid farewell to home and mother. Some feared
the destruction of the battle - field ; the wiser
feared hardship and disease ; and others, more
than all, the destruction of morals and everything good and pure in character. That the
fears of the last named were realized in some
cases cannot be denied; but that the general
result was demoralization can be denied, and
the contrary demonstrated.

Let us consider the effect of camp-life upon a
pure and noble boy ; and to make the picture
complete, let us go to his home and witness the
parting. The boy is clothed as a soldier. His
pockets and his haversack are stored with little conveniences made by the loving hands of
mother, sister, and sweetheart, and the sad yet
proud hour has arrived. Sisters, smiling through
their tears, filled with commingled pride and

sorrow, kiss and embrace their great hero. The mother, with calm heroism suppressing her tender maternal grief, impresses upon his lips a fervent, never-to-be-forgotten kiss, presses him to her heart, and resigns him to God, his country, and his honor. The father, last to part, presses his hand, gazes with ineffable love into his bright eyes, and, fearing to trust his feelings for a more lengthy farewell, says, " Good-by, my boy; God bless you ; be a man ! "

Let those scoff who will ; but let them know that such a parting is itself a new and wonderful power, a soul-enlarging, purifying, and elevating power, worth the danger, toil, and suffering of the soldier. The sister's tears, the father's words, the mother's kiss, planted in the memory of that boy, will surely bring forth fruit beautiful as a mother's love.

As he journeys to the camp, how dear do all at home become!   Oh, what holy tears he sheds!   His heart, how tender!   Then, as he nears the line, and sees for the first time the realities of war, the passing sick and weary, and the wounded and bloody dead, his soldier spirit is born ; he smiles, his chest expands, his eyes brighten, his heart swells with pride. He hurries on, and soon stands in the magic circle around the glowing fire, the admired and loved pet of a dozen true hearts. Is he happy ? Aye !

Never before has he felt such glorious, swelling, panting joy. He's a soldier now! He is put on guard. No longer the object of care and solicitude he stands in the solitude of the night, himself a guardian of those who sleep. Courage is his now. He feels he is trusted as a man, and is ready at once nobly to perish in the defense of his comrades.

He marches. Dare he murmur or complain? No; the eyes of all are upon him, and endurance grows silently, till pain and weariness are familiar, and cheerfully borne. At home he would be pitied and petted; but now he must endure, or have the contempt of the strong spirits around him.

He is hungry, — so are others; and he must not only bear the privation, but he must divide his pitiful meal, when he gets it, with his comrades; and so generosity strikes down selfishness. In a thousand ways he is tried, and that by sharp critics. His smallest faults are necessarily apparent, for, in the varying conditions of the soldier, every quality is put to the test. If he shows the least cowardice he is undone. His courage must never fail. He must be manly and independent, or he will be told he's a baby, ridiculed, teased, and despised. When war assumes her serious dress, he sees the helplessness of women and children, he hears their piteous appeals, and chivalry burns him, till he does his utmost of sacrifice and effort to protect, and comfort, and cheer them.

It is a mistake to suppose that the older men in the army encouraged vulgarity and obscenity in the young recruit ; for even those who themselves indulged in these would frown on the first show of them in a boy, and without hesitation put him down mercilessly. No parent could watch a boy as closely as his mess-mates did and could, because they saw him at all hours of the day and night, dependent on himself alone, and were merciless critics, who demanded more of their *protégé* than they were willing to submit to themselves.

The young soldier's piety had to perish ignominiously, or else assume a boldness and strength which nothing else could so well impart as the temptations, sneers, and dangers of the army. Religion had to be bold, practical, and courageous, or die.

In the army the young man learned to value men for what they were, and not on account of education, wealth, or station ; and so his attachments, when formed, were sincere and durable, and he learned what constitutes a man and a desirable and reliable friend. The stern demands upon the boy, and the unrelenting criticisms of the mess, soon bring to mind the

14

gentle forbearance, kind remonstrance, and loving counsels of parents and homefolks; and while he thinks, he weeps, and loves, and reverences, and yearns after the things against which he once strove, and under which he chafed and complained. Home, father, mother, sister, —oh, how far away; oh, how dear! Himself, how contemptible, ever to have felt cold and indifferent to such love! Then, how vividly he recalls the warm pressure of his mother's lips on the forehead of her boy! How he loves his mother! See him as he fills his pipe from the silk-embroidered bag. There is his name embroidered carefully, beautifully, by his sister's hand. Does he forget her? Does he not now love her more sincerely and truly and tenderly than ever? Could he love her quite as much had he never parted; never longed to see her and could not; never been uncertain if she was safe; never felt she might be homeless, helpless, insulted, a refugee from home? Can he ever now look on a little girl and not treat her kindly, gently, and lovingly, remembering his sister? A boy having ordinary natural goodness, and the home supports described, and the constant watching of men, ready to criticise, could but improve. The least exhibition of selfishness, cowardice, vulgarity, dishonesty, or meanness of any kind, brought down the dislike of

every man upon him, and persistence in *any one*
disreputable practice, or habitual laziness and
worthlessness, resulted in complete ostracism,
loneliness, and misery ; while, on the other
hand, he might, by good behavior and genuine
generosity and courage, secure unbounded love
and sincere respect from all.

Visits home, after prolonged absence and
danger, open to the young soldier new treasures
— new, because, though possessed always, never
before felt and realized.   The affection once
seen only in every-day attention, as he reaches
home, breaks out in unrestrained vehemence.
The warm embrace of the hitherto dignified
father, the ecstatic pleasure beaming in the
mother's eye, the proud welcome of the sister,
and the wild enthusiasm even of the old black
mammy, crowd on him the knowledge of their
love, and make him braver, and stronger, and
nobler.   He 's a hero from that hour!   Death
for these, how easy !

The dangers of the battle-field, and the demands upon his energy, strength, and courage,
not only strengthen the old, but almost create
new, faculties of mind and heart.   The death,
sudden and terrible, of those dear to him, the
imperative necessity of standing to his duty
while the wounded cry and groan, and while
his heart yearns after them to help them, the

terrible thirst, hunger, heat, and weariness, —
all these teach a boy self-denial, attachment to
duty, the value of peace and safety ; and, instead of hardening him, as some suppose they
do, make him pity and love even the enemy
of his country, who bleeds and dies for *his*
country.

The acquirement of subordination is a useful one, and that the soldier perforce has ; and
that not in an abject, cringing way, but as
realizing the necessity of it, and seeing the result of it in the good order and consequent ef-
fectiveness and success of the army as a whole,
but more particularly of his own company and
detachment. And if the soldier rises to office,
the responsibility of command, attention to detail and minutiæ, the critical eyes of his sub-
ordinates and the demands of his superiors, all
withdraw him from the enticements of vice,
and mould him into a solid, substantial character, both capable and willing to meet and overcome difficulties.

The effect of out-door life on the physical
constitution is undoubtedly good, and as the
physical improves the mental is improved ; and
as the mind is enlightened the spirit is enno-
bled. Who can calculate the benefit derived
from the contemplation of the beautiful in nature, as the soldier sees ? Mountains and val-

leys, dreary wastes and verdant fields, rivers, sequestered homes, quiet, sleepy villages, as they lay in the morning light, doomed to the flames at evening; scenes which alternately stir and calm his mind, and store it with a panorama whose pictures he may pass before him year after year with quiet pleasure. War is horrible, but still it is in a sense a privilege to have lived in time of war. The emotions are never so stirred as then. Imagination takes her highest flights, poetry blazes, song stirs the soul, and every noble attribute is brought into full play.

It does seem that the production of one Lee and one Jackson is worth much blood and treasure, and the building of a noble character all the toil and sacrifice of war. The camp-fires of the Army of Northern Virginia were not places of revelry and debauchery. They often exhibited scenes of love and humanity, and the purest sentiments and gentlest feelings of man were there admired and loved, while vice and debauch, in any from highest to lowest, were condemned and punished more severely than they are among those who stay at home and shirk the dangers and toils of the soldier's life. Indeed, the demoralizing effects of the late war were far more visible " at home," among the skulks and bomb-proofs and suddenly diseased, than in the army. And the demoralized men

of to-day are not those who served in the army.
The defaulters, the renegades, the bummers and
cheats, are the boys who enjoyed fat places and
salaries and easy comfort; while the solid, respected, and reliable men of the community are
those who did their duty as soldiers, and, having learned to suffer in war, have preferred to
labor and suffer and earn, rather than steal, in
peace.

And, strange to say, it is not those who suffered most and lost most, fought and bled, saw
friend after friend fall, wept the dead and
buried their hopes, — who are now bitter and
dissatisfied, quarrelsome and fretful, growling
and complaining; no, they are the peaceful,
submissive, law - abiding, order - loving, of the
country, ready to join hands with all good men
in every good work, and prove themselves as
brave and good in peace as they were stubborn
and unconquerable in war.

Many a weak, puny boy was returned to his
parents a robust, healthy, *manly man*. Many
a timid, helpless boy went home a brave, independent man. Many a wild, reckless boy went
home sobered, serious, and trustworthy. And
many whose career at home was wicked and
blasphemous went home changed in heart, with
principles fixed, to comfort and sustain the old
age of those who gave them to their country,

not expecting to receive them again.   Men learned that life was passable and enjoyable without a roof or even a tent to shelter from the storm ; that cheerfulness was compatible with cold and hunger ; and that a man without money, food, or shelter need not feel utterly hopeless, but might, by employing his wits, find something to eat where he never found it before ; and feel that, like a terrapin, he might make himself at home wherever he might be. Men did actually become as independent of the imaginary " necessities " as the very wild beasts. And can a man learn all this and not know better than another how to economize what he has, and how to appreciate the numberless superfluities of life ?   Is he not made, by the knowledge he has of how little he really needs, more independent and less liable to dishonest exertions to procure a competency ?

If there were any true men in the South, any brave, any noble, they were in the army.   If there are good and true men in the South now, they would go into the army for similar cause. And to prove that the army demoralized, you must prove that the men who came out of it are the worst in the country to-day.   Who will try it ?

Strange as it may seem, religion flourished in the army.   So great was the work of the chaplains that whole volumes have been written to describe the religious history of the four years of war. Officers who were ungodly men found themselves restrained alike by the grandeur of the piety of the great chiefs, and the earnestness of the humble privates around them. Thousands embraced the Gospel, and died triumphing over death. Instead of the degradation so dreaded, was the strange ennobling and purifying which made men despise all the things for which they ordinarily strive, and glory in the sternest hardships, the most bitter self-denials, cruel suffering, and death. Love for home, kindred, and friends, intensified, was denied the gratification of its yearnings, and made the motive for more complete surrender to the stern demands of duty. Discipline, the cold master of our enemies, never caught up with the gallant devotion of our Christian soldiers, and the science of war quailed before the majesty of an army singing hymns.

Hypocrisy went home to dwell with the able-bodied skulkers, being too closely watched in the army, and too thoroughly known to thrive. And so the camp-fire often lighted the pages of the best Book, while the soldier read the orders of the Captain of his salvation. And often did the songs of Zion ring out loud and clear on the cold night air, while the muskets rattled and

the guns boomed in the distance, each intensi-
fying the significance of the other, testing the
sincerity of the Christian while trying the courage of the soldier.   Stripped of all sensual
allurements, and offering only self-denial, pa-
tience, and endurance, the Gospel took hold of

the deepest and purest motives of the soldiers,
won them thoroughly, and made the army as
famous for its forbearance, temperance, respect
for women and children, sobriety, honesty, and
morality as it was for endurance and invincible
courage.

Never was there an army where feeble old

age received such sympathy, consideration, and protection. Women, deprived of their natural protectors, fled from the advancing hosts of the enemy, and found safe retreat and chivalrous protection and shelter in the lines of the Army of Northern Virginia. Children played in the camps, delighted to nestle in the arms of the roughly-clad but tender-hearted soldiers. Such was the behavior of the troops on the campaign in Pennsylvania, that the citizens of Gettysburg have expressed wonder and surprise at their perfect immunity from insult, violence, or even intrusion, when their city was occupied by and in complete possession of the Boys in Gray.

CHAPTER XII.

THE CONFEDERATE BATTLE-FLAG.

THIS banner, the witness and inspiration of many victories, which was proudly borne on every field from Manassas to Appomattox, was conceived on the field of battle, lived on the field of battle, and on the last fatal field ceased to have place or meaning in the world. But the men who followed it, and the world which watched its proud advance or defiant stand, see in it still the unstained banner of a brave and generous people, whose deeds have outlived their country, and whose final defeat but added lustre to their grandest victories.

It was not the flag of the Confederacy, but simply the banner, the battle-flag, of the Confederate soldier. As such it should not share in the condemnation which our *cause* received, or suffer from its downfall. The whole world can unite in a chorus of praise to the gallantry of the men who followed where this banner led.

It was at the battle of Manassas, about four o'clock of the afternoon of the 21st of July, 1861, when the fate of the Confederacy seemed trembling in the balance, that General Beauregard, looking across the Warrenton turnpike, which passed through the valley between the position of the Confederates and the elevations beyond occupied by the Federal line, saw a body of troops moving towards his left and the Federal right. He was greatly concerned to know, but could not decide, what troops they were, whether Federal or Confederate. The similarity of uniform and of the colors carried by the opposing armies, and the clouds of dust, made it almost impossible to decide.

Shortly before this time General Beauregard had received from the signal officer, Captain Alexander, a dispatch, saying that from the signal station in the rear he had sighted the colors of this column, drooping and covered with the dust of journeyings, but could not tell whether they were the Stars and Stripes or the Stars and Bars. He thought, however, that they were probably Patterson's troops arriving on the field and reënforcing the enemy.

General Beauregard was momentarily expecting help from the right, and the uncertainty and anxiety of this hour amounted to anguish. Still the column pressed on. Calling a staff officer, General Beauregard instructed him to go at once to General Johnston, at the Lewis House, and say that the enemy were receiving

HERE ARE THE COLORS!

heavy reënforcements, that the troops on the plateau were very much scattered, and that he would be compelled to retire to the Lewis House, and there re-form, hoping that the troops ordered up from the right would arrive in time to enable him to establish and hold the new line.

Meanwhile, the unknown troops were pressing on. The day was sultry, and only at long intervals was there the slightest breeze. The colors of the mysterious column hung drooping on the staff. General Beauregard tried again and again to decide what colors they carried. He used his glass repeatedly, and handing it to others begged them to look, hoping that their eyes might be keener than his.

General Beauregard was in a state of great anxiety, but finally determined to hold his ground, relying on the promised help from the right; knowing that if it arrived in time victory might be secured, but feeling also that if the mysterious column should be Federal troops the day was lost.

Suddenly a puff of wind spread the colors to the breeze. It was the Confederate flag, — the Stars and Bars ! It was Early with the Twenty-Fourth Virginia, the Seventh Louisiana, and the Thirteenth Mississippi. The column had by this time reached the extreme right of the Federal lines. The moment the flag was recognized, Beauregard turned to his staff, right and left, saying, " See that the day is ours ! " and ordered an immediate advance.   In the mean time Early's brigade deployed into line and charged the enemy's right; Elzey, also, dashed upon the field, and in one hour not an enemy was to be seen south of Bull Run.

While on this field and suffering this terrible anxiety, General Beauregard determined that the Confederate soldier must have a flag so distinct from that of the enemy that no doubt should ever again endanger his cause on the field of battle.

Soon after the battle he entered into correspondence with Colonel William Porcher Miles, who had served on his staff during the day, with a view to securing his aid in the matter, and proposing a blue field, red bars crossed, and gold stars.

They discussed the matter at length.   Colonel Miles thought it was contrary to the law of heraldry that the ground should be blue, the bars red, and the stars gold.   He proposed that the ground should be red, the bars blue, and the stars white.   General Beauregard approved the change, and discussed the matter freely with General Johnston.   Meanwhile it became known that designs for a flag were under discussion, and many were sent in.   One came from Mississippi; one from J. B. Walton and E. C. Hancock, which coincided with the design of Colonel Miles. The matter was freely discussed at headquarters, till, finally, when he arrived at Fairfax Court House, General Beauregard caused his draughtsman (a German) to make drawings of all the various designs which had been submitted. With these designs before them the officers at headquarters agreed on the famous old banner, — the red field, the blue cross, and the white stars. The flag was then submitted to the War Department, and was approved.

The first flags sent to the army were presented to the troops by General Beauregard in person, he then expressing the hope and confidence that they would become the emblem of honor and of victory.

The first three flags received were made from "*ladies' dresses*" by the Misses Carey, of Baltimore and Alexandria, at their residences and the residences of friends, as soon as they could get a description of the design adopted. One of the Misses Carey sent the flag she made to General Beauregard. Her sister presented hers to General Van Dorn, who was then at Fairfax Court House. Miss Constance Carey, of Alexandria, sent hers to General Joseph E. Johnston.

General Beauregard sent the flag he received

at once to New Orleans for safe keeping. After the fall of New Orleans, Mrs. Beauregard sent the flag by a Spanish man-of-war, then lying in the river opposite New Orleans, to Cuba, where it remained till the close of the war, when it was returned to General Beauregard, who presented it for safe keeping to the Washington Artillery, of New Orleans.

This much about the battle-flag, to accomplish, if possible, two things : first, preserve the little history connected with the origin of the flag ; and, second, place the *battle* flag in a place of security, as it were, separated from all the political significance which attaches to the *Confederate* flag, and depending for its future place solely upon the deeds of the armies which bore it, amid hardships untold, to many victories.